Teen Stress

Recent Titles in
Q&A Health Guides

TEEN STRESS

❖❖

Your Questions Answered

Nicole Neda Zamanzadeh and Tamara D. Afifi

Q&A Health Guides

BLOOMSBURY ACADEMIC
NEW YORK • LONDON • OXFORD • NEW DELHI • SYDNEY

BLOOMSBURY ACADEMIC
Bloomsbury Publishing Inc
1385 Broadway, New York, NY 10018, USA
50 Bedford Square, London, WC1B 3DP, UK
29 Earlsfort Terrace, Dublin 2, Ireland

BLOOMSBURY, BLOOMSBURY ACADEMIC and the Diana logo
are trademarks of Bloomsbury Publishing Plc

First published in the United States of America by ABC-CLIO 2020
Paperback edition published by Bloomsbury Academic 2024

Library of Congress Cataloging-in-Publication Data
Names: Zamanzadeh, Nicole Neda, author. | Afifi, Tamara D., author.
Title: Teen stress : your questions answered / Nicole Neda Zamanzadeh and Tamara D. Afifi.
Description: Santa Barbara, California : Greenwood, an imprint of ABC-CLIO,
LLC, [2020] | Series: Q&A health guides | Includes bibliographical references and index.
Identifiers: LCCN 2020011107 (print) | LCCN 2020011108 (ebook) |
ISBN 9781440865589 (hardcover) | ISBN 9781440865596 (ebook)
Subjects: LCSH: Stress in adolescence. | Teenagers—Mental health.
Classification: LCC BF724.3.S86 Z36 2020 (print) |
LCC BF724.3.S86 (ebook) | DDC 155.5/182—dc23
LC record available at https://lccn.loc.gov/2020011107
LC ebook record available at https://lccn.loc.gov/2020011108

ISBN: HB: 978-1-4408-6558-9
PB: 979-8-7651-2961-6
ePDF: 978-1-4408-6559-6
eBook: 979-8-2161-5397-9

Series: Q&A Health Guides

To find out more about our authors and books visit www.bloomsbury.com
and sign up for our newsletters.

Contents

Series Foreword

All of us have questions about our health. Is this normal? Should I be doing something differently? Whom should I talk to about my concerns? And our modern world is full of answers. Thanks to the Internet, there's a wealth of information at our fingertips, from forums where people can share their personal experiences to Wikipedia articles to the full text of medical studies. But finding the right information can be an intimidating and difficult task—some sources are written at too high a level, others have been oversimplified, while still others are heavily biased or simply inaccurate.

Q&A Health Guides address the needs of readers who want accurate, concise answers to their health questions, authored by reputable and objective experts, and written in clear and easy-to-understand language. This series focuses on the topics that matter most to young adult readers, including various aspects of physical and emotional well-being as well as other components of a healthy lifestyle. These guides will also serve as a valuable tool for parents, school counselors, and others who may need to answer teens' health questions.

All books in the series follow the same format to make finding information quick and easy. Each volume begins with an essay on health literacy and why it is so important when it comes to gathering and evaluating health information. Next, the top five myths and misconceptions that surround the topic are dispelled. The heart of each guide is a collection of questions and answers, organized thematically. A selection of five case studies provides real-world examples to illuminate key concepts. Rounding out each volume are a directory of resources, glossary, and index.

It is our hope that the books in this series will not only provide valuable information but will also help guide readers toward a lifetime of healthy decision making.

Acknowledgments

Stress can feel lonely. It can feel and be difficult to overcome, but this book is written for and about you and your ability to handle, learn, and grow with stress. Whether that stress is occurring to you now or happened in the past, I firmly believe—based on my personal and professional experience—it is never too late or too early to learn more about yourself. Teen stress does not only affect teens it also affects their teachers, nurses, doctors, parents or guardians, siblings, family members, and friends. Moreover, teens' stresses today are often carried into adulthood. So, whomever you are and whatever situation or feeling drew you to be curious about teens stress, thank you for taking the step of potentially helping yourself and others. My hope is that this book sheds light on your experiences or those of people you love and that you can use this knowledge to identify, accept, and act upon your feelings.

I want to thank my support system—the many people who helped me accomplish this lifelong goal of writing a book and on the importance of teenage years. The encouragement of friends (Victoria, Amanda, Katie, Britney, Bahar, Nahal, Sarah Jasmine, Will, and Paula); family members, especially my sister Davina; mentors, including my coauthor, Tammy, and my partner, Jarrett, was invaluable to me. I am so grateful for their willingness to listen to my feelings throughout the process, discuss their own stresses as teens, go to coffee shops to write with me, read through chapters, and provide feedback throughout the process. Their interest and involvement not only motivated the completion of the book during life challenges but also improved the quality of the writing and content in the book.

I am grateful for Maxine Taylor, the editor of this book, who has had patience with me through this challenging but rewarding process. I appreciate ABC-CLIO for recognizing the importance of this topic and helping circulate information that aims to improve the lives of youth and adults.

Finally, I dedicate this book to the many adults and teens who helped me confront and cope with my teen stress. I hope that I am paying it forward!

> *You are imperfect, you are wired for struggle, but you are worthy of love and belonging.*
> – Brené Brown

Introduction

Adolescents have always experienced stress, but there are indicators that they may be more stressed now than ever before. For instance, the rise of anxiety and depressive symptoms. I have noticed this shift among my undergraduate and graduate students over the last twenty years. It has hit a critical point like I have never seen before. In fact, the University of California, Los Angeles (UCLA), recently brought together researchers, administrators, and university counselors in the summer of 2019 for its first resilience and mental health summit to talk about the mental health crisis across the University of California (UC) campuses. Counseling and psychological services across the UC campuses are bursting at the seams, and the universities are ill-equipped to help the number of students who need assistance.

The statistics support the feeling that professors, administrators, and clinicians have on college campuses. For instance, in a recent National Survey on Drug Use and Mental Health (2018), researchers surveyed six hundred thousand adults over a ten-year period, from 2009 to 2019, and found that young adults aged twenty to twenty-one had the largest increases in psychological distress than any other age group, and it increased by 78 percent over the past decade. Even though college students are considered by researchers to be older adolescents or emerging adults, mental health has become a public health crisis throughout the adolescent years (ages ten to twenty-two). The statistics on the rise of psychological distress among junior high and high school students mirrors that of college-age students.

This book comes at an important time. As a researcher who studies family communication, stress, and adolescence, I want to know why adolescents are so stressed. One of the contributors to their stress appears be social media and smartphones. Even though social media is an important and primary way adolescents maintain their friendships, a significant number of studies now show the negative effect of social media on adolescent mental health. The chapters in this book talk about issues such as the fear of missing out and social comparisons that adolescents make because of social media. Again, these issues always existed for teenagers but technology seems to have increased how often it occurs and how intensely teens feel it.

Other factors include the current culture surrounding politics and race. People are also more polarized in their political identities and attitudes. Racism has always existed, but people have more avenues for communicating their racism today than years prior, which can make vulnerable groups of adolescents particularly stressed. Moreover, there is increased societal pressure to get into college and to pay for college tuition, which places various pressures on teenagers and their parents. Teens feel they need excellent grades, extra advanced placement classes, volunteer activities, and entrance exams preparation so that they can get into a good college. Meanwhile, one quarter of all adolescents do not have enough food to eat each day. And, their parents may be working more than one job to make ends meet.

Finally, adolescents today care about the world around them. They are concerned about the environment and the impact of climate change. They are humanitarians. They are concerned about gun control. Today's adolescents are growing up with active shooter drills; as opposed to their parents who may have only experienced drills for natural disasters when they were in school. Some schools are currently being built with bullet-proof glass as a part of the architectural plan to protect against school shooters. These are the types of stressors that define this generation. Adolescents are attempting to manage all of these stressors simultaneously. The chapters in this book address many of the issues that adolescents face today.

More importantly, as a parent of two teenage girls, ages thirteen and fifteen, I want to know what we can do about it. How can parents help their adolescents feel happy, secure, and safe? What can adolescents do to learn to manage their stress themselves? How can teens develop a positive psychological well-being? This book provides crucial, practical information for teenagers, parents, clinicians, and teachers and administrators alike about the stress that adolescents are experiencing and how they can manage it. It provides a timely glimpse into the world of teens. The book also dispels common myths that people have about stress and teens. In the end, readers will leave the book with a better understanding of what stress is and how it reveals itself in adolescence—and with hope for how to effectively manage it going forward.

Tamara D. Afifi, professor
Department of Communication
University of California, Santa Barbara

Guide to Health Literacy

On her 13th birthday, Samantha was diagnosed with type 2 diabetes. She consulted her mom and her aunt, both of whom also have type 2 diabetes, and decided to go with their strategy of managing diabetes by taking insulin. As a result of participating in an after-school program at her middle school that focused on health literacy, she learned that she can help manage the level of glucose in her bloodstream by counting her carbohydrate intake, following a diabetic diet, and exercising regularly. But, what exactly should she do? How does she keep track of her carbohydrate intake? What is a diabetic diet? How long should she exercise and what type of exercise should she do? Samantha is a visual learner, so she turned to her favorite source of media, YouTube, to answer these questions. She found videos from individuals around the world sharing their experiences and tips, doctors (or at least people who have "Dr." in their YouTube channel names), government agencies such as the National Institutes of Health, and even video clips from cat lovers who have cats with diabetes. With guidance from the librarian and the health and science teachers at her school, she assessed the credibility of the information in these videos and even compared their suggestions to some of the print resources that she was able to find at her school library. Now, she knows exactly how to count her carbohydrate level, how to prepare and follow a diabetic diet, and how much (and what) exercise is needed daily. She intends to share her findings with her mom and her aunt, and now she wants to create a chart that summarizes what she has learned that she can share with her doctor.

Samantha's experience is not unique. She represents a shift in our society; an individual no longer views himself or herself as a passive recipient of medical care but as an active mediator of his or her own health. However, in this era when any individual can post his or her opinions and experiences with a particular health condition online with just a few clicks or publish a memoir, it is vital that people know how to assess the credibility of health information. Gone are the days when "publishing" health information required intense vetting. The health information landscape is highly saturated, and people have innumerable sources where they can find information about practically any health topic. The sources (whether print, online, or a person) that an individual consults for health information are crucial because the accuracy and trustworthiness of the information can potentially affect his or her overall health. The ability to find, select, assess, and use health information constitutes a type of literacy—health literacy—that everyone must possess.

THE DEFINITION AND PHASES OF HEALTH LITERACY

One of the most popular definitions for health literacy comes from Ratzan and Parker (2000), who describe *health literacy* as "the degree to which individuals have the capacity to obtain, process, and understand basic health information and services needed to make appropriate health decisions." Recent research has extrapolated health literacy into health literacy bits, further shedding light on the multiple phases and literacy practices that are embedded within the multifaceted concept of health literacy. Although this research has focused primarily on online health information seeking, these health literacy bits are needed to successfully navigate both print and online sources. There are six phases of health information seeking: (1) Information Need Identification and Question Formulation, (2) Information Search, (3) Information Comprehension, (4) Information Assessment, (5) Information Management, and (6) Information Use.

The first phase is the *information need identification and question formulation phase*. In this phase, one needs to be able to develop and refine a range of questions to frame one's search and understand relevant health terms. In the second phase, *information search*, one has to possess appropriate searching skills, such as using proper keywords and correct spelling in search terms, especially when using search engines and databases. It is also crucial to understand how search engines work (i.e., how search results are derived, what the order of the search results means, how to use the snippets that are provided in the search results list to select websites, and how to determine which listings are ads on a search engine results page). One also has to limit reliance on surface characteristics, such as the design of a website or a book (a website or book that appears to have a lot of information or looks aesthetically pleasant does not necessarily mean it has good information) and language used (a website or book that utilizes jargon, the keywords that one used to conduct the search, or the word "information" does not necessarily indicate it will have good information). The next phase is *information comprehension*, whereby one needs to have the ability to read, comprehend, and recall the information (including textual, numerical, and visual content) one has located from the books and/or online resources.

To assess the credibility of health information (*information assessment* phase), one needs to be able to evaluate information for accuracy, evaluate how current the information is (e.g., when a website was last updated or when a book was published), and evaluate the creators of the source—for example, examine site sponsors or type of sites (.com, .gov, .edu, or .org) or the author of a book (practicing doctor, a celebrity doctor, a patient of a specific disease, etc.) to determine the believability of the person/ organization providing the information. Such credibility perceptions tend to become generalized, so they must be frequently reexamined (e.g., the belief that a specific news agency always has credible health information needs continuous vetting). One also needs to evaluate the credibility of the medium (e.g., television, Internet, radio, social media, and book) and evaluate—not just accept without questioning—others' claims regarding the validity of a site, book, or other specific source of information. At this stage, one has to "make sense of information gathered from diverse sources by identifying misconceptions, main and supporting ideas, conflicting information, point of view, and biases" (American Association of School Librarians [AASL], 2009, p. 13) and conclude which sources/ information are valid and accurate by using conscious strategies rather than simply using intuitive judgments or "rules of thumb." This phase is the most challenging segment of health information seeking and serves as a determinant of success (or lack thereof) in the information-seeking process. The following section on Sources of Health Information further explains this phase.

The fifth phase is *information management*, whereby one has to organize information that has been gathered in some manner to ensure easy retrieval and use in the future. The last phase is *information use*, in which one will synthesize information found across various resources, draw conclusions, and locate the answer to his or her original question and/ or the content that fulfills the information need. This phase also often involves implementation, such as using the information to solve a health problem; make health-related decisions; identify and engage in behaviors that will help a person to avoid health risks; share the health information found with family members and friends who may benefit from it; and advocate more broadly for personal, family, or community health.

THE IMPORTANCE OF HEALTH LITERACY

The conception of health has moved from a passive view (someone is either well or ill) to one that is more active and process based (someone is working toward preventing or managing disease). Hence, the dominant focus has shifted from doctors and treatments to patients and prevention, resulting in the need to strengthen our ability and confidence (as patients and consumers of health care) to look for, assess, understand, manage, share, adapt, and use health-related information. An individual's health literacy level has been found to predict his or her health status better than age, race, educational attainment, employment status, and income level (National Network of Libraries of Medicine, 2013). Greater health literacy also enables individuals to better communicate with health care providers such as doctors, nutritionists, and therapists, as they can pose more relevant, informed, and useful questions to health care providers. Another added advantage of greater health literacy is better information-seeking skills, not only for health but also in other domains, such as completing assignments for school.

SOURCES OF HEALTH INFORMATION: THE GOOD, THE BAD, AND THE IN-BETWEEN

For generations, doctors, nurses, nutritionists, health coaches, and other health professionals have been the trusted sources of health information. Additionally, researchers have found that young adults, when they have health-related questions, typically turn to a family member who has had firsthand experience with a health condition because of their family member's close proximity and because of their past experience with, and trust in, this individual. Expertise should be a core consideration when consulting a person, website, or book for health information. The credentials and background of the person or author and conflicting interests of the author (and his or her organization) must be checked and validated to ensure the likely credibility of the health information they are conveying. While books often have implied credibility because of the peer-review process involved, self-publishing has challenged this credibility, so qualifications of book authors should also be verified. When it comes to health information, currency of the source must also be examined. When examining health information/studies presented, pay attention to the exhaustiveness of research methods utilized to offer recommendations or conclusions. Small and nondiverse sample size is often—but not always—an indication of reduced credibility. Studies that confuse correlation with causation is another potential issue to watch for. Information seekers must also pay attention to the sponsors of the research studies. For example, if a study is sponsored by manufacturers of drug Y and the study recommends that drug Y is the best treatment to manage or cure a disease, this may indicate a lack of objectivity on the part of the researchers.

The Internet is rapidly becoming one of the main sources of health information. Online forums, news agencies, personal blogs, social media sites, pharmacy sites, and celebrity "doctors" are all offering medical and health information targeted to various types of people in regard to all types of diseases and symptoms. There are professional journalists, citizen journalists, hoaxers, and people paid to write fake health news on various sites that may appear to have a legitimate domain name and may even have authors who claim to have professional credentials, such as an MD. All these sites *may* offer useful information or information that appears to be useful and relevant; however, much of the information may be debatable and may fall into gray areas that require readers to discern credibility, reliability, and biases.

While broad recognition and acceptance of certain media, institutions, and people often serve as the most popular determining factors to assess credibility of health information among young people, keep in mind that there are legitimate Internet sites, databases, and books that publish health information and serve as sources of health information for doctors, other health sites, and members of the public. For example, MedlinePlus (https://medlineplus.gov) has trusted sources on over 975 diseases and conditions and presents the information in easy-to-understand language.

The chart here presents factors to consider when assessing credibility of health information. However, keep in mind that these factors function only as a guide and require continuous updating to keep abreast with the changes in the landscape of health information, information sources, and technologies.

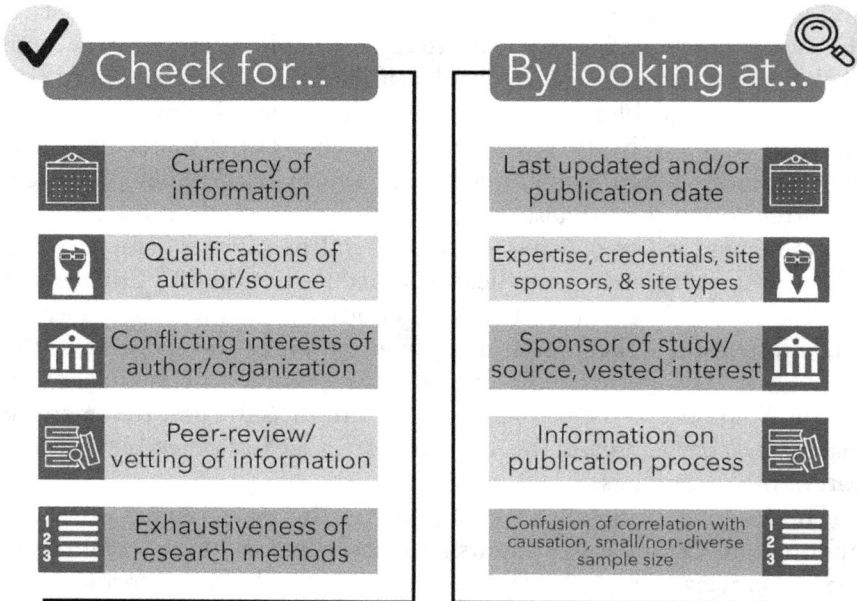

Check for...	By looking at...
Currency of information	Last updated and/or publication date
Qualifications of author/source	Expertise, credentials, site sponsors, & site types
Conflicting interests of author/organization	Sponsor of study/ source, vested interest
Peer-review/ vetting of information	Information on publication process
Exhaustiveness of research methods	Confusion of correlation with causation, small/non-diverse sample size

All images from flaticon.com

The chart can serve as a guide; however, approaching a librarian about how one can go about assessing the credibility of both print and online health information is far more effective than using generic checklist-type tools. While librarians are not health experts, they can apply and teach patrons strategies to determine the credibility of health information.

With the prevalence of fake sites and fake resources that appear to be legitimate, it is important to use the following health information assessment tips to verify health information that one has obtained (St. Jean et al., 2015, p. 151):

- **Don't assume you are right:** Even when you feel very sure about an answer, keep in mind that the answer may not be correct, and it is important to conduct (further) searches to validate the information.
- **Don't assume you are wrong:** You may actually have correct information, even if the information you encounter does not match—that is, you may be right and the resources that you have found may contain false information.
- **Take an open approach:** Maintain a critical stance by not including your preexisting beliefs as keywords (or letting them influence your choice of keywords) in a search, as this may influence what it is possible to find out.

- **Verify, verify, and verify:** Information found, especially on the Internet, needs to be validated, no matter how the information appears on the site (i.e., regardless of the appearance of the site or the quantity of information that is included).

Health literacy comes with experience navigating health information. Professional sources of health information, such as doctors, health care providers, and health databases, are still the best, but one also has the power to search for health information and then verify it by consulting with these trusted sources and by using the health information assessment tips and guide shared previously.

Mega Subramaniam, PhD
Associate Professor, College of Information
Studies, University of Maryland

REFERENCES AND FURTHER READING

American Association of School Librarians (AASL). (2009). *Standards for the 21st-century learner in action.* Chicago, IL: American Association of School Librarians.

Hilligoss, B., & Rieh, S.-Y. (2008). Developing a unifying framework of credibility assessment: Construct, heuristics, and interaction in context. *Information Processing & Management, 44*(4), 1467–1484.

Kuhlthau, C. C. (1988). Developing a model of the library search process: Cognitive and affective aspects. *Reference Quarterly, 28*(2), 232–242.

National Network of Libraries of Medicine (NNLM). (2013). Health literacy. Bethesda, MD: National Network of Libraries of Medicine. Retrieved from nnlm.gov/outreach/consumer/hlthlit.html

Ratzan, S. C., & Parker, R. M. (2000). Introduction. In C. R. Selden, M. Zorn, S. C. Ratzan, & R. M. Parker (Eds.), *National Library of Medicine current bibliographies in medicine: Health literacy.* NLM Pub. No. CBM 2000-1. Bethesda, MD: National Institutes of Health, U.S. Department of Health and Human Services.

St. Jean, B., Taylor, N. G., Kodama, C., & Subramaniam, M. (February 2017). Assessing the health information source perceptions of tweens using card-sorting exercises. *Journal of Information Science.* Retrieved from http://journals.sagepub.com/doi/abs/10.1177/0165551516687728

St. Jean, B., Subramaniam, M., Taylor, N. G., Follman, R., Kodama, C., & Casciotti, D. (2015). The influence of positive hypothesis testing on youths' online health-related information seeking. *New Library World*, *116*(3/4), 136–154.

Subramaniam, M., St. Jean, B., Taylor, N. G., Kodama, C., Follman, R., & Casciotti, D. (2015). Bit by bit: Using design-based research to improve the health literacy of adolescents. *JMIR Research Protocols*, *4*(2), paper e62. Retrieved from http://www.ncbi.nlm.nih.gov/pmc /articles/PMC4464334/

Valenza, J. (2016, November 26). Truth, truthiness, and triangulation: A news literacy toolkit for a "post-truth" world [Web log]. Retrieved from http://blogs.slj.com/neverendingsearch/2016/11/26/truth-truthiness -triangulation-and-the-librarian-way-a-news-literacy-toolkit-for-a -post-truth-world

---
❖❖❖

Common Misconceptions about Teen Stress

1. TEENS AREN'T STRESSED; THEY'RE JUST "SEEKING ATTENTION"

Teens experience real stress. This is because stress is a natural reaction we all have to challenges, and it plays a role in the way people grow and learn throughout life. Adults may wonder whether teens are looking for attention or acting out rather than feeling stressed. Their inconsistencies and intense reactions may appear inauthentic or fake. However, research on teens suggests that it is often because teens are struggling to cope with and communicate their stress that leads them to engage in more risky and unpredictable behavior. Their inability to deal with stress may motivate attention-seeking behavior, but this is typically a signal that they need help.

Getting help can be complicated for teenagers. The teenage years are filled with a desire for more independence, which can make it difficult for teens to accept or ask for help. Teens can be in denial of their stress, unaware, or ashamed of what is causing their stress. This makes it especially challenging for them to get the support they may need. Research on stress reveals it is the result of a challenging situation as well as a result of a person views of the situation. For instance, some people find completing math problems really stressful because they are not or feel they are not skilled (or good) at it, while others enjoy it. The amount of stress a person feels is related to how big of a challenge it is for that individual. Thus, research suggests that it is *not* accurate nor fair to compare stress by comparing situations.

The best way to know whether an event or experience is stressful for a person is to understand how that person perceives it and what strategies that person uses to cope with it. The myth that teens are not stressed but are simply seeking attention or evading challenges can be harmful. Unfortunately, judgments and criticisms of a teen's stress can increase its intensity. It can add to the challenge of coping with stress by reducing teens chances of asking for, finding, or using support and solutions to their problems.

For more information about what stress is, see question 1.

2. ADULTS AND TEENS EXPERIENCE STRESS IN THE SAME WAY

It is true that adults and teens both experience stress; however, the intensity and clarity of their experiences of stress (i.e., knowing or understanding that they are stressed) differs. This myth has been busted by developmental psychologists (those who study the ways people change throughout their lifetime) who have revealed that different stages of life are related to unique biological and psychological capacities and challenges. Although adults and teens both experience stress due to obstacles in their lives, they experience stress for different reasons and in different ways. Because of their developing minds and bodies, teens are faced with many new challenges. In comparison to childhood, teens begin to develop romantic feelings for others as well as the ability to look inward and reflect on what role they should play in the world. These challenges are often already resolved or are at least familiar by the time people become adults. The number of new situations teens experience increases the likelihood of stress and the difficulty of coping with stress. Beyond the different situations that adults and teens consider a hardship, they also differ in their mental and physical maturity. Adults are usually more stable—their minds and bodies do not change as much until advanced age. The exploratory state of teens' sense of self often interferes with their ability to evaluate how well they can cope with and overcome some of their challenges. These various factors reduce emotional clarity and stability, demonstrating how teen stress differs from adult stress.

To learn more about the differences between teen and adult stress, please see question 5.

3. TEEN STRESS IS FRIVOLOUS; THEY SWEAT THE "SMALL" STUFF

Teen stress is not only real but also highly significant; the habits teenagers gain and learn when faced with stress can have long-term consequences. Just because a person is a teenager does not mean that they do not experience difficult challenges. Teenagers can be faced with some of the most difficult stressors of any age group: loss, abuse, addiction, toxic relationships, and health issues are just a few examples. Yet, some of their challenges are specific to their particular stage of life. Teens are only beginning to gain the capacity for perspective taking (i.e., seeing the world from someone else's eyes) and for planning (i.e., thinking about the future). Meanwhile, they are trying to uncover their identities—who they are and what value they bring to the world. Thus, teens need guidance through their new challenges and mistakes, or the situations they think are mistakes. They often do not know how to evaluate the potential harm or benefits of their behavior.

These challenges of teenage years are essential in the process of becoming well-adjusted and well-functioning adults. Their experiences of stress and the ways they learn to cope with stress help them become resilient adults who can adapt to and overcome various challenges. Research has demonstrated that learning better coping tools for stress at a younger age leads to more positive responses to stress in the future. In other words, when teens recognize stress and try various ways of dealing with it, they are learning skills for adulthood. On the other hand, if the stressors of the teenage years are not coped with, psychologically denied or hidden away, they have the potential of creating more challenges in adulthood. Through understanding stress and how to cope with stress, teens can learn and grow.

Questions 9–28 examine some of the most common causes of teen stress.

4. STRESS IS ALWAYS BAD

Believe it or not, stress can actually be good. Challenges are unavoidable and can be healthy components of life. For instance, teens' stress can play a role in building skills that can be transferred to other challenging situations as they age. Overcoming stress builds self-confidence and good support systems—which involves knowing whom to trust and when to trust them. Some researchers have even demonstrated that stress may improve mental and physical abilities for the short term. During some challenges, such as an exam or a sports game, our minds and bodies become stronger and more focused due to stress induced increased energy. Stress can even led to positive emotions, such as hope, gratitude, and accomplishment (i.e., believing that because a person successfully achieved one goal, they will meet other goals).

Finally, some researchers find that there can be two types of stress: (1) *eustress*, viewing stressors in a positive way, which is also known as good stress, and (2) *distress*, viewing stress as something highly negative. Games or adventures can cause eustress and are often viewed as fun challenges, whereas people in distress feel challenges (e.g., a car accident, an exam, a break up, an illness) are overwhelming and exhausting. People can sometimes experience distress and eustress together. The reason people feel eustress or distress depends not only on the situation they experience but also on the resources they have and their perception of the situation. Thus, while stress is usually thought of as something negative that can harm teens, it can also play an essential role in positive experiences of growth, self-esteem, and hope. Unfortunately, the perpetuation of this myth that "stress is bad" has stigmatized many individuals' experiences of stress, often making the stress worse. Stress is natural—yes, it can be difficult or painful, but it can also be rewarding and worthwhile.

The positive sides of stress are explored more in question 2.

5. TEEN STRESS IS A NEW PHENOMENON

Teen stress is not novel. Studies of stress began in the 1920s. Since then, the concept has progressively become a part of modern life and daily conversation. Similarly, researchers in the early 1900s recognized the teenage years as distinguishable from childhood and adulthood. Yet, being a "teenager" has only really become a part of our collective understanding in the last fifty years. For these reasons, the challenges of the teen years—ages thirteen to nineteen—are still being explored. Even though we often use the term *teenager* to refer to these years, some psychologists believe that, developmentally, this stage of life can be extended to as young as ten and as old as twenty-four years. The society in which teenagers live continues to change and create new challenges for this developmental stage (i.e., this period of mental and biological growth). Thus, while the occurrence of teenage stress is not new, it is changing.

It is important to understand how the sources of stress transform to acknowledge, validate, and support teenagers through their obstacles so they may become healthy and resilient adults. When adults perpetuate the notion that teen stress is new, they unintentionally communicate to teenagers that their experiences are not normal. Because teens are developing their identities and understanding their roles in society, feeling abnormal can be detrimental to their self-confidence and well-being. Belittling, stigmatizing, or making teens feel as though their experience of stress is not normal increases teen stress and makes it more harmful.

Question 6 takes a closer look at how teen stress has changed over time.

QUESTIONS AND ANSWERS

General Information

1. What is stress?

People often use the word *stressed* to describe how they are feeling, but what exactly is stress? Stress is the reaction of the mind and body to difficult, upsetting, or unsettling events or situations.

Stress has developed as a necessary reaction to potential threats in life. These threats can be anything seen as dangerous to a person's survival or needs. Today, stress is also an outcome of new challenges or difficult situations. The intensity or the amount of stress a person feels depends on the perceived difficulty of the problem being experienced and whether they believe it can be overcome. If a challenge becomes too difficult to manage, it causes distress and the feeling of being overwhelmed or fatigued.

Evolutionary psychologists argue that stress was originally a response that helped protect people from predators and dangerous situations that may have led to death. With society's advancement, people now feel stress when other important needs are threatened, such as a sense of belonging or financial safety. Threats to self-esteem or relationships can also feel very dangerous. When people cannot deal with their challenges or are unsure about it, they will feel stressed.

In 1984, Richard Lazarus and Susan Folkman, pioneers in the study of stress, defined stress as an individual's reaction to challenges in their environment. In their theory, *cognitive appraisal*, the way a person thinks about and judges their environment, is relevant to their well-being. Specifically, the way people evaluate their problems and their ability to prevent harm or deal with these challenges explains how much stress they feel and how it affects their health. Their developmental stage or age, previous experiences, and personality traits may lead people to see more situations as threats and cause them to feel more stress. When individuals can engage in empathy, emotional expression, and creative problem-solving in dealing with obstacles, they are better able to reduce the resulting stress.

For teenagers, threats to reputations and relationships can be particularly stressful. This is because of the mental, emotional, and physical changes caused by puberty (the period in which boys and girls become sexually mature). Puberty involves changes in hormones—the substances that regulate people's bodies—and thus changes in teens' minds and bodies. These changes lead to increased sensitivity about how others view them and where they belong in their world. Anything that makes it difficult to maintain a positive reputation or self-esteem may be viewed as an intense threat. With few skills to deal with stress-related and hormone-related increases in the amount and range of their emotions, teens may feel that they do not know how to deal with stress or may act impulsively as a reaction to the stress.

People experience stress on three levels. First, stress affects people mentally and emotionally—this involves their feelings and thoughts. Second, stress affects people physically, which is the way people feel in their bodies. Third, stress occurs physiologically, meaning there are changes to the organs, blood, or tissues inside people's bodies. Mentally and emotionally, stress can include having negative thoughts and emotions, such as sadness, loneliness, and anxiety. Negative thoughts can include, "I can't do it" or "No one likes me." Physically, stress can cause an individual's palms to start sweating, their heart to beat faster, and even tightness in their chest. Finally, physiologically, stress can impact the endocrine system (which produces the body's hormones), the digestive system (which processes food), and the immune system (which protects the body from disease).

Cortisol, the body's stress hormone, can be over- or underproduced when a person is in a challenging situation. Cortisol is produced every day to energize the body, especially in the morning, but it is also released when a person feels threatened or in danger. The release of cortisol increases energy in the body to fight or face the issue or to flee or avoid the challenge. This is commonly referred to as the fight-or-flight response. After dealing with the cause of stress, the body adjusts its output of cortisol. When the body is exposed to high levels of cortisol for a long period of time, however, the way the body reacts to stress can change. As a result, the person may feel tired, have headaches, or stomach pain.

Stress does not only happen during a challenge. It can also happen in anticipation of a challenge or even after the challenge has passed. This anticipation for the future or reflecting on the past may increase the stress and its negative effects. Preparation for a public speech, a tough conversation, or a test, for instance, may include fears of experiencing rejection or failure threatening their self-esteem and relationship. A person may imagine making a mistake in front of a crowd, having a huge fight, or getting a bad grade. In other words, people can feel stress because they predict they will be in tough situations before they even experience them.

Similarly, people may continue to think about a hardship after it has passed, for example, continuing to think about how they failed a test or how they lost a close loved one. When people continue to think about their challenges, they continue to experience the stress of the threat even after it has passed. This is referred to as *rumination*. Thinking about threatening experiences can lead the mind and body to react as though the situation is happening again and again.

2. How can teenage stress ever be good?

Stress is neither good nor bad; it is a natural part of everyday life. Rather, the way teens respond to stress can *create* positive or negative outcomes. Through the ways that teens deal with stress, they can learn new skills and build confidence. Teens who experience stress have found benefits in overcoming their challenges, including becoming more resilient to future obstacles.

A large body of research suggests that stress has the ability to lead teenagers to learn and grow. Stress can become motivating and create a sense of pride or mastery when teenagers accomplish something difficult, even if that accomplishment was simply coping with their own fears. Teenagers report that the self-understanding and self-confidence they create in managing stress are the two most prominent factors that create eustress, or positive emotions toward stress. Research by Richard Lerner, professor in applied developmental science at Tufts University and the director of the Institute for Applied Research in Youth Development, reports that teens are both affecting and being affected by their environments. Positive and negative experiences of stress are not only a result of the types of challenges teens experience but also a reflection of their culture, friends, family, and communities. Teens who are more resilient or who experience more eustress are also likely to have an environment that helps them be more resilient.

However, some challenges—such as illnesses, death, and assault—are more likely to cause distress and are therefore generally identified as traumas. These are more stressful situations. Most individuals experience at least one trauma in their lives; however, the type and number of traumas teens experience determine the impact they may have on their health. Research reveals that the stress experienced as a result of trauma can still create an opportunity for posttraumatic growth. Instances of posttraumatic growth are the positive changes that result from the struggle with trauma. Trauma is still difficult and painful, but this research suggests that teens learn through coping with this stress. David Meyerson, PhD, a developmental neuropsychologist, recently reviewed some existing studies and summarized that there are five ways teens achieve growth after trauma: (1) they see new possibilities, (2) they relate better to others, (3) they feel more personal strength, (4) they have a greater appreciation of life, and (5) they experience spiritual change. These new perspectives and skill sets improve teens' quality of life.

Research suggests that when teens experience hope, optimism, and support, they are more likely to also have positive emotions due to stress as well as posttraumatic growth. Stress can be good when teenagers have been practicing a positive mindset toward challenges, when they *feel* they have support from friends and loved ones, and when they frequently receive guidance, acknowledgment, and validation from their friends and loved ones. When teenagers are able to experience eustress, they protect their health and are less likely to experience distress in the future.

Scientists who study the *sensitization hypothesis* among animals (e.g., birds, rodents) as well as humans argue that stress can improve attention, memory, and problem-solving abilities. These scientists have found that, in the short term, a little bit of stress, especially eustress can improve test scores and theatrical performances. The energy eustress generates can temporarily boost attention and memory but may still hinder control, the ability to restrain or stop behaviors. For those who have regularly experienced stress, especially in early life, they may only experience this advantage in other stressful circumstances because of sensitization.

Nonetheless, the research clearly suggests that stress can have its benefits. It does not discount or completely dissipate the harms of stress, but the advantages of stress are often overlooked. Growth, as a result of stress, is most likely to occur when teens are able to engage in emotional expression, receive social support, feel acceptance, and learn coping skills from the adults and friends surrounding them as they overcome challenges.

3. What indicates a teen is experiencing stress?

Because there are various causes and types of stress, people express their stress in various ways. Someone's stress can be shown or indicated physically (in the way a person's body feels), physiologically (inside a person's body), mentally (in a person's thoughts), emotionally (in a person's feelings), or behaviorally (in the ways a person acts). These feelings or behaviors may include regularly feeling tired, having tightness in the chest or stomachaches, having sad or angry thoughts, feeling fear, or neglecting personal hygiene. Some indicators of stress may be easily recognized by the stressed person, but others may be more noticeable to friends or loved ones.

When people are stressed, they may notice changes to their bodies, such as getting sick more frequently, having a stomachache every day, having a headache, or feeling like they have too much or too little energy. People may realize how stressed they are after visiting their doctor and perhaps seeing that they have high blood pressure, symptoms of anxiety, or more inflammation in their stomach. They may also notice that they cannot stop thinking about something that happened yesterday or something they think will happen tomorrow. They may even notice they are stressed because they are having more negative thoughts about themselves.

There are many signals that can help to identify someone who is stressed. One way to identify stress is to notice the person's facial expressions, body language, and the words they use. For instance, people who are stressed smile less often, do not look into people's eyes, physically shake, breathe heavily, slouch, or put their hands on their face. People who are stressed are also likely to say things like, "I don't know if I can do this," "I wish I could just sleep for days," "Nothing seems to be going my way," and "I am so annoyed."

Teens who are stressed may also be more frequently distracted, uninterested, frustrated, or upset, especially by their own or other's mistakes or judgements. A sign of stress may be that the person struggles to pay attention in conversations at lunch with friends, at sport practices or theater rehearsals, during dinner with family, or in the classroom at school. Thus, stress can be often signaled by someone performing worse at school. Teens who are stressed are often more quickly frustrated and overwhelmed and thus quicker to shed tears. They may be especially sensitive or more likely to get angry or sad due to being criticized or judged by friends, teachers, or family members. Because stress impacts energy and focus, researchers find that over time people who are more stressed are more likely to make mistakes and have a hard time processing others' negative comments afterward.

Sometimes it is easier to see a teen's stress by the actions that show they are trying to deal with stress. For example, stress is highly related to more frequent and increased drug, marijuana, tobacco, and alcohol use; internet or video game addiction; and obesity. Most of the research reveals that when people are overwhelmed, especially for prolonged periods, they may rely or depend on other substances, behaviors, or food to help cope. These behaviors are often used for numbing or avoiding the pain of stress and quickly become unhealthy tools. Another behavior that reveals teens may be coping with stress is that they begin to withdraw from friends or socially isolate themselves. They may stop going to school, practices, family outings, dinner or lunch with friends, or friends' houses, birthday parties, or sleepovers. This often occurs because the stress causes them to feel shame or embarrassment, and thus it reduces their desire to see other people.

Not all indicators of stress are negative or obvious. Some people who are stressed may try to combat their stress with frequent positivity and smiles. Sometimes stress is indicated by teen's ambitions or their goals: they may have multiple projects or clubs at school or want to get a makeover or buy new things. These again may be signs of teens coping with the stress of developing their identity or aiming to get into college. The cause of stress can also be a positive change: getting a new job, starting at a new school, dating someone new, moving, or even becoming the leader of a club or organization. Even when there are no negative feelings directly attached to these experiences, people are likely to experience stress due to new challenges.

Stress is a part of daily life and not always a negative experience. By using the indicators of stress, it is possible to at least label it when it is happening and then begin to think about how to deal with it.

4. What's the difference between acute and chronic stress?

Acute and *chronic* refer to the characteristics of a situation that contribute to when and how much stress a person feels. Acute stress is sudden, usually intense, and caused by a specific event. Chronic stress results from events or situations that are ongoing. The two differ in the ways they impact health and the best ways to cope with them.

Whether a challenge is acute or chronic depends on its nature and on the characteristics of the person coping with it. When stress is acute, it is caused by a single event that had a sudden onset and was extremely difficult or overwhelming. When stress is chronic, the challenge may occur over time through reoccurring situations or ongoing problems. Chronic stress may be less difficult or intense in each instance of the problem, but it may become equally harmful, depending on how frequent and how long the issue continues.

All teens experience stress, but the types of challenges they encounter vary widely. These incidents can range in their duration (the length of time), frequency (the number of instances), and severity (the intensity or difficulty) of the obstacles they face. Managing a potentially difficult situation, such as having an enduring illness such as type 1 diabetes, living with a sibling who has a mental health disorder, being bullied at school, or experiencing violence in a romantic or sexual relationship can lead to reoccurring challenges known as chronic stress. On the other hand, the hardships experienced, such as the death of a loved one, a move, a divorce, a car accident, or a natural disaster in a teen's hometown, may occur only once, but the stress can be very intense, known as acute stress.

However, some obstacles can create both acute and chronic stress. This may be the case for those who survive traumatic events, such as emotional, sexual, or physical abuse. Although a traumatic situation may have initially led to acute stress, the psychological consequences of the trauma may last for years after the experience has ended. This is common for those who have symptoms of or have been diagnosed with posttraumatic stress disorder (PTSD). In this case, the trauma also creates chronic stress. This may be true in other circumstances as well. For instance, a loved one being diagnosed with schizophrenia or cancer may cause acute stress, but coping with the challenges of that diagnosis produces chronic stress. The reverse situation is also possible. The chronic stress of coping with an emotionally abusive romantic partner or toxic friend can lead to acute stress when ending one's relationships with that person.

Although these terms help to classify different stressors (causes of stress), it is not always clear which of the two is occurring. The terms *acute* and *chronic* are used to normalize the experiences of stress and help researchers study how stress differs from person to person. The research in this area suggests there is variation in the way acute and chronic stressors impact people. This may depend on whether the acute or chronic challenge is more physical or psychological. It may also differ depending on whether the adversity comes from within the person's body and mind, as is the case with a disease, or occurs due to the person's environment, such as the divorce of parents.

A challenge may become more acute and chronic if a person ruminates and feels embarrassed or ashamed. In other words, the stigma teens feel toward their situations can increase the likelihood and harm caused by either form of stress. This can happen with both acute stressors, such as the loss of a family member, as well as chronic stressors, such as an enduring disease. Similarly, resources such as money, time, access to good health care, quality of relationships, and knowledge about how to overcome the stress all impact a teen's likelihood to experience acute and chronic stress.

Although acute stress can be harmful, the detrimental effects may be contained to a single period of one's life. People may overcome the challenge and thus return to their typical life. However, this is less likely among teenagers. As stressors become more chronic, they could begin to experience negative biological effects, such as increased exhaustion or fatigue and negative moods. Chronic stressors can often become more harmful than acute stressors. Frequent bouts of stress can fatigue someone's ability to recover, leading to irreversible damage. These situations are extreme. Yet, teens can often reverse the negative consequences of stress. They may even be able to grow as a result of acute or chronic stress by learning new skills for overcoming future challenges and gaining a new perspective that leads to more gratitude and happiness.

5. How is the stress that teens feel different from the stress adults experience?

Teens' stress differs from adults' stress not only because of differences in experience and age but also because of their different mental and emotional capacities, maturity, and internal stability. Teenagers are in a unique life phase; they are not quite adults, but they are also no longer children. Because of this ambiguity, the transition can be tumultuous; the changes to teens' biology and environment leave them vulnerable to stress.

The teenage years are classically thought of as a time full of conflict with parents, emotional disruptions, and risk-taking. In 1904, the developmental American psychologist G. Stanley Hall claimed these feelings and behaviors were outcomes of increased emotional intensity and reduced self-regulation (a person's ability to monitor, evaluate, and change their actions) in a theory called *storm and stress*. Hall claimed the problems of teenage years are different from that of adults because teens experience more intense feelings and yet have less capability to react to them. The storm and stress approach to defining the teen years suggested that all children would inevitably become moody rebels and in turn put themselves at risk. This theory became a part of popular culture, did not help researchers understand the experiences of teenagers.

Since then, scientists have found that there is a lot more variation in teens' development. Studies reveal that teens undergo hormonal, neuronal, and structural changes that increase their ability to reflect on feelings and identity and to increase their sensitivity to other people's perceptions, sexuality, and friendships. While biological changes that increase emotional intensity and less behavioral control are inevitable as causes of teen stress, teen stress is better explained by the interaction between teens' environment—that is, their family dynamics, their social status, their exposure to trauma—and their biology. Teenagers' environment impacts how difficult it is for them to learn how to manage their own emotions. Studies find that an earlier and faster onset of puberty and other physical changes leads to greater challenges for teenagers largely because they may feel more shame and less support from friends.

Teen stress is unique because their biology causes them to have more challenges in their relationships. For instance, they are sensitive to the ways they are perceived by friends and potential romantic partners as well as their teachers, mentors, and family. Many of these challenges are novel and thus require new skills for problem-solving and emotional management, such as calming down a broken heart, dealing with confusion about one's sexuality, or dealing with feeling betrayed by a friend. These new experiences occur with a more intense emotional response for teens than they might for adults.

Teens are also challenged by identifying and expressing their emotions; they are still learning the language that helps them understand their own feelings. Because teens are less capable of recognizing, managing, and communicating their emotions, their stress can begin to snowball. Feeling embarrassed by friends can raise a lot of emotions. If these feelings are not soothed, these emotions can spill over into other situations, leading to an unrelated argument at home with parents. These emotions can grow more intense if teens do not get validation, trusted advice, or just a space to share their inner thoughts and feelings.

Adults can struggle with managing their emotions or knowing themselves in similar ways as teens. Still, teens do not have as much experience or ability to understand themselves, freedom, or financial resources as adults. Teens may not be more stressed than adults, but the impacts of their stress can be more long lasting. Teenage and adult stress differ, but they are also related. Many adults' stress relates to their teen experiences and the subsequent outcomes of their own meaning making, identity development, and coping skills gained in their teens years.

6. How does teen stress today differ from the past?

Some of the reasons and ways teens experience stress today are the same as the past, but there are also some reasons and ways that they differ. Teen stress has transformed over the decades as awareness about stress as well as mental health has increased—in other words, people have become more aware of stress. Teen stress is transforming because the definition of a teenager has evolved. Teens' stress differs in that social expectations and parenting techniques have changed. Technology has also impacted the ways and reasons teens feel stress.

Recent statistics of reported American teenage stress, depression (a mental health disorder that leads to long-lasting feelings of sadness and lost interest), and anxiety (the feeling of worry that can become a mental health disorder when fear or nervousness becomes long-lasting and frequent) reveal consistent increases such that teens' well-being has become a public health concern. Many professionals, parents, and teens have begun to wonder about teenagers' experiences and the causes of the rise in their stress. There are many factors that contribute to teen stress and why the rate of reported teen stress has risen. What are the potential reasons for this increasing statistic? What may be the causes?

Teenage stress may be different today because teens may have a greater capability and opportunity to recognize and report that they feel stress. Stress and teenagers as terms are each only a century old—originating in 1920 and 1900, respectively. Scientists began to study teenagers in the 1950s, though interest in the teenage years really became popular in the 1960s. Then, in 1980s, the youth development movement began to think about how to help teens become healthy adults.

Since then, schools and parents have become more concerned or interested in understanding their teens as a unique life stage. They have also become more involved in supporting teens through their challenges, such as peer pressure to use drugs or drink and drive or to give up and drop out of school. Today, American knowledge and societal values have changed, leading more people to gain insights into the stress in teens' lives that may have once been overlooked, unexpressed, or mislabeled. Teens can also easily educate themselves today about stress and mental health via the internet. There are more resources to help them identify their stress.

Importantly, research and learning about teen stress is an ongoing process. The increasing reports of anxiety and depression are leading scientists such as Denny Borsboom, a philosopher of measurement and professor in Australia, to revisit earlier definitions of disorders or illnesses such as depression and anxiety. It is impossible to know whether the current definitions of *stress* and *knowledge of this definition* would impact the rates of teenage stress and mental health issues in the past. This is especially salient given that many teenagers in the past may have been drafted into wars and potentially returned as veterans who had experienced trauma and developed mental health issues as adults. It is also important to remember that while depression and anxiety have increased, teenagers are engaging in less drug and alcohol use as well as crime than before.

Relatedly, around the globe as well as in the United States, the definition of *teenage years* has been appropriately increased to ages ten to twenty-four to account for the different ways people develop. These changes, in addition to the reduced child-mortality rates (i.e., rates of death in children) due to improved modern medicine, have led to a global all-time high in teenage population. Altogether, this means more people are being categorized as teenagers, teenagers have more power to understand their own feelings, and more adults are interested and understanding of the feelings and thoughts that teens communicate. Yet, teenagers still experience great stigma around their stress. Although the trend is in the right direction, many teenagers find their family, siblings, and other adults in their life may undermine or belittle their challenges, which makes their stress worse by not guiding teens to cope. Other adults may make teens' stress worse by feeling overwhelmed by it, ignoring it, communicating that stress is bad, or comparing teens' stress to their own stress at their age.

In addition to these factors, changes in parenting practices have transformed, potentially contributing to stress. In the 1980s, developmental psychologists John Bowlby and Mary Ainsworth identified that a trustworthy and supportive relationship between parents and children positively impacts their self-concept and their views of others as teens. These secure relationships lead to less anxiety and depressive symptoms in adulthood. Many experts encouraged parenting practices to be revised to focus more heavily on building a more trustworthy and positive relationship with their children.

In response to these findings, some parents have aimed to create a more trustworthy and supportive relationship through praise to increase their teens' self-esteem or by protecting teens from challenges altogether. Research suggests that teenagers who hear unrealistic or only positive statements from their parents (e.g., "You're the best" or "You are perfect in every way") or who regularly feel overprotected by their parents often lose trust and emotional closeness with their parents or themselves. Scholars believe that teens may learn that they are only loveable when they are "good" and that mistakes are not tolerable. This may result in perfectionism and an increased likelihood to experience depressive or anxious symptoms. Parenting improved with increased expressions of love and positive affirmations, but this alone does not create a good parent-child relationship.

The reasons teenagers feel stress have also changed. Teenagers today may feel stressed academically because the expectations for obtaining jobs have transformed. Teens may feel pressured to have more secondary education after high school, which is very expensive, and feel they must perform better. The requirements for obtaining a higher education, such as a bachelor's, master's, or professional degree, have also become more difficult. Teenagers may work while also attending school and engaging in extracurricular activities, such as sports, volunteering, clubs, or theater or musical groups.

Another potential factor that causes teen stress to differ today is the existence of technology, such as smartphones and social media. One of the most obvious and rapid changes in teenagers' lives is their access and ownership of portable internet-connected devices. Teens today are more exposed to the stress around their environment. They experience unique forms of stress caused by an increased reliance on technology, their constant accessibility to their friends, and the hostile content on the internet, known as digital stress. Research suggests that the increase in technology use happened at the same time as increases in rates of mood disorders and suicidality. There is also some evidence that time spent on "screen activities," such as playing a video game, surfing the internet, texting friends, and posting on social media, has been associated with greater loneliness and depression. But, most research reveals it is the type of use that matters most.

The causes of teenage stress are constantly evolving. Yet, the underlying reasons teenagers feel stress may be the same as many years ago. Teen stress is a reaction to the new experiences they have, their developing sexuality, their forming identity, the increased intensity of emotions, range of emotions, need for belonging beyond their family, and desire to become independent. Teenage stress likely existed far before anyone scientifically labeled it, and the youth of the past were able to adapt. Those adaptations may have been beneficial and/or harmful. Today, the challenge is to identify the new adversities facing youth and to use our knowledge of stress and teen development to help current and future generations of teenagers.

7. What is digital stress?

Digital stress is the term for the overwhelming and exhausting challenges that are created by digital technologies. The online environment that is constantly available through portable devices creates easy access to information and other people. While this has been beneficial, it has also created personal, social, and cultural obstacles. These difficulties and dilemmas are considered digital causes of stress.

Digital stress is difficult to measure directly. However, in 2019, a nationally representative survey of American by Common Sense Media found that almost three out of four teens (72%) believe that technology companies manipulate teens to spend more time on their devices. Almost half of the teens (~50%) reported feeling frustrated at how often their friends spend time on their phones as opposed to spending time together. A third (33%) of teens reported that their parents seemed obsessed with their devices and that they wished that they spent less time on them.

Research on the topic of digital stress is still being conducted as society continues to develop greater dependencies on internet-connected devices. Existing findings demonstrate the potentially overwhelming nature of digital life. There are two ways that scientists theorize (or have logically concluded) people experience digital stress. First, digital stress can be an outcome of increased aggression and relational closeness. Second, digital stress is a part of the process of learning how to best use new devices.

Emily Weinstein and Robert Selman, two researchers at the Harvard Graduate School of Education, studied the first theory. To them, digital stress includes having hostile and aggressive interactions or being exposed to violent content. This can include having a debate or conflict, experiencing public humiliation, receiving hostile messages, or reading a post that demonstrates hatred toward a group of people. Digital stress also includes the risks and tensions from having both an offline and online self because of constantly being or feeling the pressure to be accessible. This may include managing online personas and accounts and the risk of being hacked.

For teens, digital stress can be a daily experience. Since it has become a normalized part of their social routine, still they may not always be aware of the effect digital stress has on their lives. The complications of managing the amount of time spent online or on devices may not feel overwhelming every day; rather, they exhaust teens over time. However, the aggression and level of pressure that teens experience from their online social networks can become harmful. When the hostility and cruel comments become repetitive or grow in volume, they become less and less tolerable. Cyberbullying, or cybervictimization, combines both forms of digital stress and is more likely to decrease mental and physical health.

In 2018, Emily Weinstein, PhD, shared that teens have created a few strategies that help deal with digital stress. These included getting help from others (parents, friends, legal authorities, or school officials), communicating directly or confronting people who are causing digital stress, cutting ties with people who cause digital stress, ignoring or avoiding dangerous situations, and utilizing digital solutions such as reporting fake profiles and negative content. These strategies particularly recommend getting help when experiencing aggression and hostility such as bullying as well as cutting ties with or ignoring and avoiding people who pressure teens to always be available.

Other researchers find that technology leads to stress because teens have conflicting feelings about their devices. In 2018, researchers found that these conflicts are felt personally and socially. Young adults feel technology can be stimulating, entertaining, and enjoyable through its ability to connect with others, but it can also be exhausting to monitor all that information. They also found that the access to many websites and applications makes it easy to lose track of time, and yet it can also include helpful tools for managing their school notes and schedules. It is becoming easier to make plans through technology, but it is also easier for plans to get canceled—leaving schedules in more chaos. Perhaps most importantly, teens felt technology helped them create more relationships and talk more frequently with friends and family, but these relationships generally felt less intimate. Digital stress thus appears to be partially an outcome of learning how to use technology and coping with the limitations and benefits of devices.

Regardless of which approach one takes to digital stress, teenagers are particularly at risk of experiencing digital stress. Many teens can feel digital stress due to the interactions they have with friends online or on their devices as well as the arguments they have with their family members about their device use. Their privacy may not only feel threatened by friends but also by family members. Unfortunately, digital stress can lead to increased secrecy due to the shame, embarrassment, or fear of losing the ability to use their devices, decreasing the likelihood of teens seeking help from parents or other adults.

8. Is stress contagious?

Stress may not be contagious in the same way that a virus or bacteria can be spread from one person to another, but when an individual is exposed to other people's stress—either directly through interacting with them or indirectly through watching videos or reading news and social media posts—they may feel stressed themselves. This is because humans are highly empathetic.

Over the last decade, the American Psychological Association (APA) has tracked how stress has increased across the generations in the United States. In a 2018 survey, the APA found that less than half of Generation Z (current teens) report having good mental health. Many teens report that they are stressed about mass shootings, rising rates of suicide, global warming, the deportation of immigrant and migrant families, and widespread sexual harassment and assault reports. Teens' heightened concern about national issues suggests that their increased access to information has increased their stress about the world. This is likely because teens' access to information about the world is no longer largely filtered by parents or teachers or limited to the people in close proximity. Thus, by being exposed to more of the stress in the world, they too experience more stress.

Beyond the impact of having access to information from billions of people around the world via the internet, teens are still likely to interact with close friends and family who may also be experiencing stress. Challenges naturally occur at all points in life, and most people encounter someone in their life who is experiencing stress. Infants, toddlers and children are unlikely to be able to identify and overcome stress alone, but they do not need to do so; their developmental stage and needs allow them to be more dependent on their parents and siblings. However, the teenage years involve increased empathy, a greater variety of emotions, *and* a desire for independence that becomes necessary in adulthood. This suggests they are more likely to feel others' stress, be surrounded by stress, and, yet, have less support to cope with stress.

Stress researchers have noted that because humans experience empathy for one another, they often share in each other's emotions. Empathy is defined by two components. The first includes the ability to take on another person's perspective and think about their experiences. This is a cognitive, or mental, form of empathy. Empathy also involves concern and care for the well-being of another person. This second component involves having emotional sensitivities to the experiences of others. Empathy—whether cognitive, emotional, or both—explains why one person's stress can lead to another person's experience of stress.

Teens' increased cognitive empathy caused by changes to their brain explains why they are more vulnerable to experiencing other people's stress than children. Researchers find that emotional empathy is likely stable across a person's lifetime and exists at a very young age. Infants as young as eight months old will begin to cry if they are in the presence of another crying baby or even a crying adult. As they get closer to twelve months of age, they may even try to offer help. These studies demonstrate that children recognize crying as a sign of stress and emotionally empathize; they react automatically, even without an understanding of stress. Beginning in the teenage years and throughout life, people continue to become more aware and able to identify when they feel each other's stress.

Cognitive empathy first appears when children develop a sense of self versus others, also known as the *theory of mind*. Soviet psychologist Lev Vygotsky discovered that the concept of theory of mind first appears at eight years of age and then undergoes a massive transformation during the teenage years. Developmental psychologists who have investigated the changes in the brain, found that during teenage years the part of the brain known as the frontal lobe, which is involved in the ability to think abstractly—grows. The frontal lobe contributes to the ability to plan and make decisions as well as the ability to take another person's perspective, leading to cognitive empathy.

As cognitive empathy develops and emotional empathy becomes more fine-tuned, they create new and complex challenges. The growth in empathy is met with a lack of experience in the skillful use of empathy and ability to label emotions. Being able to understand the value of empathy and to apply it toward decision-making evolves over many years and often depends on a teen's identity. Teenagers may feel stress in reaction to a friend or family member's problem and find it challenging to decide how to respond. Scientists currently believe that the frontal lobe involved in empathy, reflection, and planning is not fully developed until around ages twenty-eight to thirty.

Although stress can be "contagious," it is not necessarily harmful. Shared stress can still be beneficial for teens. It can motivate them to help one another, deepen relationships, and teach them to cope with a challenge by experiencing a friend's struggle with it. Scholars applying Vygotsky's theory of social development argue that children and teens learn more about their emotions and how to cope with stress from friends than from adults. Therefore, while stress may be contagious, coping may be as well. Through empathy, teenagers can become resources for each other, contributing to and building up mutual resilience.

Sources of Teen Stress

9. What is bullying? How can bullying and cyberbullying cause teen stress?

Bullying and cyberbullying are aggressive acts that become repetitive and create feelings of helplessness in the victim. They threaten teen safety and can ultimately reduce the number of people a teen can rely on to help them deal with their stress. Thus, frequent and more intimidating or violent forms of bullying can result in delinquent behavior, social anxiety, eating disorders (e.g., anorexia, bulimia, and obesity), depression, and suicide.

The United States seems to have equivalent bullying levels as other countries, and bullying rates are increasing globally and creating a concern for teens' health. Traditional verbal bullying is still the most frequent and common form of aggression. In 2015, the National Center for Education Statistics (NCES), a governmental agency dedicated to investigating educational outcomes in the United States, found that 21 percent of students between the ages of twelve and eighteen had experienced bullying at school during the school year. Of these students, 33 percent said they were bullied at least once or twice a month. The NCES found no difference in bullying between students in private and public schools.

Common Sense Media, a nonprofit organization dedicated to understanding the impact of media, conducted a survey with a nationally representative sample of U.S. teens. Of these teenagers, aged thirteen to seventeen years, 10 percent reported experiencing cyberbullying at least once, with the majority reporting that the bullying was somewhat serious. However, almost 50 percent of teens reported observing cyberbullying. Other research by the Cyberbullying Research Center in 2016 suggests that cyberbullying is far more common; it found that about one in three (33%) middle school and high school students report having been a victim. Female students; those who identify as lesbian, gay, bisexual, transgender, or queer (LGBTQ); and teens from minority ethnicities report experiencing more bullying victimization.

Bullying involves repetitively and intentionally inflicting harm on another person. It includes verbal, physical, relational (i.e., harming relationships or a victim's reputation), and property-damaging forms of aggression. Verbal aggression may include teasing, name calling, sexual commenting, and threatening. Pushing, hitting, slapping, and kicking are forms of physical aggression. Relational aggression can occur through spreading rumors or lies and by isolating, excluding, or leaving out someone from a group. Finally, property-damaging includes stealing, changing, or borrowing someone's property, such as online accounts, devices, car, notebooks, locker, or backpack, without that person's consent.

Direct bullying happens when the bully repetitively harms the victim by speaking or touching them. Indirect bullying occurs without an interaction between the bully and the victim; it happens through communicating with other people or using property without permission. For example, indirect bullying occurs when people spread rumors about another person; online, this can include sending manipulated or edited images or hacking into one's account and posting. Both traditional bullying and cyberbullying can lead to chronic high-intensity or severe stress. Some bullying behaviors are considered crimes, including harassment, hazing, and assault.

There are some important distinctions between bullying and cyberbullying. Traditional bullying usually occurs in person, or face-to-face, and requires an imbalance of power that favors the person engaging in the bullying. Cyberbullying involves online or digital acts of hostility that make use of the ability to remain anonymous or the ease of spreading information online. For instance, cyberbullying acts can involve sharing a message or photo to a large number of people or circulating a message for a long period of time. Cyberbullying may not always be an outcome of a clear difference in power (i.e., being more vs. less popular) and may be less intentional than traditional bullying.

Bullying victims are frequently children of strict parents. The degree to which parents are nurturing and validating predicts both who is more likely to become a bully and who is more likely to be a victim of bullying. Less supportive parents leave their teenagers more at risk for bullying. Therefore, victims of bullying frequently have lower self-esteem. Previous research suggests that the impact of bullying largely depends on the frequency and duration of the harassment. However, the challenges of coping with bullying for teens can be exacerbated or made worse by the reactions of the adults surrounding them if they are not validating or are too aggressive.

Victims of bullying often experience diminished safety and compromised mental health. Bullying can result in absences from school or sudden drops in grades because school no longer feels safe. Some students resort to carrying weapons. Bullied students are twice as likely to engage in cyberviolence or to become a bully later as they use their own aggression to try to reassert power and regain safety. Unfortunately, teens' developing emotional regulation, or ability to recognize and cope with their feelings, and need for independence, or lack of reliance on adults, make this option very dangerous. In some cases, bullying can be severely psychologically harmful, perhaps resulting in depression, eating disorders, and even suicide. The Centers for Disease Control and Prevention (CDC) reported that, in 2016, suicide was the second-leading cause of death for ages ten to twenty-four, followed by homicide.

Bullying remains a challenging topic for adults and teens alike. Parents and educators often struggle to identify the appropriate strategies for preventing bullying and protecting people who have been bullied from its harmful consequences. An immense challenge remains in deciding if, when, and how much punishment is applicable to teens who vary in the ways and reasons for bullying. Yet, the research clearly indicates that the impact of bullying, whether it is traditional or cyber, can be long lasting and harmful for teens.

10. How do revenge porn, cyberstalking, and cybersex harassment cause teen stress?

The teen body experiences many hormonal changes due to sexual maturity. These changes co-occur with changes in their mental experiences of both romantic and sexual interests. Technology has allowed for new ways of expressing and exploring these interests. Recent estimates suggest that at least 50 percent of U.S. young adults have sent a nude or seminude photo of themselves by at least the age of eighteen, and two-thirds (66%) have received these explicit photos from others. Sending nude photos and texting about performing sexual acts, potentially while masturbating, known as "sexting," is a form of pornography and can be abused and employed for sexual or romantic violence and harassment. Teens can experience harm to their mental health due to digital crimes such as revenge porn, cyberstalking, and cybersex harassment.

One of these sexually aggressive uses of digital communication involves nonconsensual pornography (NCP), commonly referred to as "revenge porn" as well as "cyber rape," or "involuntary porn." NCP is most common among teens and young adults. Revenge porn involves the sharing or distribution of sexually explicit or nude images of a person without their consent. NCP is often, shared by a previous romantic or sex partner (i.e., an ex-boyfriend or ex-girlfriend) that originally received the image to view privately with others for whom the photo was not originally intended. The term *revenge porn* refers to the abuse of these intimate photos, which upon being shared are considered porn, to inflict harm, usually by embarrassing the person in the photograph.

In 2016, Amanda Lenhart, at the Pew Research Center, found that 4 percent of teens over age fifteen, or one in twenty-five, reported that someone had threatened or had shared photos of their nude or intimate images without their consent. In 2017, the Cyber Civil Rights Initiative (CCRI) conducted a survey of U.S. young adults and found that 12.8 percent have been victimized by or threatened with NCP; of these, the majority (8%) were victims. Meanwhile, 5.2 percent reported having perpetrated NCP at some point in their lives. In both Amanda Lenhart's and in the CCRI's findings, females or women were more likely and more frequently victimized than males or men. Not all NCP is motivated by the desire to harm the other person. Sometimes it is for bragging or entertainment. The CCRI study found that 79 percent of those who inflicted NCP reported sharing the photo with friends without the intention of hurting the person. Of those who engaged in NCP, 50 percent stated that they had distributed these images via text or SMS.

Although the creation of pornography—or sexually explicit material used to excite arousal—from romantic partners' photos may not have been intended as a form of aggression, the existing research suggests that it has a long-lasting mental health impact on the victims. Those threatened or victimized by NCP experience more depression and anxiety. Revenge porn often leads to embarrassment and stress due to the reputational and relational challenges. For some victims, this led to death from suicide. Due to the gravity of the violation, forty-six states have created some form of revenge porn law to protect victims and criminalize this behavior by making it punishable by law.

Likewise, stalking is a serious crime. Legally, stalking involves behaviors directed at a person that would cause a reasonable person to feel fear. Stalking frequently includes a constellation, or connected set, of behaviors, such as repeated unwanted intrusions or interactions with another person that are perceived as threatening. Some behaviors that contribute to stalking include making unwanted calls; sending unwanted letters, e-mails, or texts; following or spying on the victim; showing up in locations or places of a victim without a legitimate reason; waiting for a victim in places; leaving unwanted items or gifts; and sharing a person's location without their consent.

Cyberstalking is the unwanted use of digital communication and online information to intrude upon a person's life that results in fear for the victim. For instance, this can involve using social media or Global Positioning System (GPS) to track or monitor a person's locations and activities in a way that creates fear for the victim. If these behaviors are repetitive but do not implicate a threat or fear, they are called cyber harassment. If they invoke fear or imply a threat, they are considered cyberstalking. Cyberstalking, or repetitive online monitoring and communication with nonconsenting individuals, violates privacy and freedom. Cyberstalking and revenge porn can occur with strangers. Yet, it most frequently occurs with acquaintances, current dating partners, or previous romantic or sexual partners. These obsessive behaviors can often last for months and even up to years.

In 2012, the U.S. Department of Justice's Bureau of Justice Statistics found that 3.3 million persons aged eighteen or older had been victims of stalking. It also found that the largest proportion of cyberstalking victims by age are teens, specifically those eighteen to nineteen years old. Most research confirms that cyberstalking often leads to physical stalking. The outcomes of cyberstalking include PTSD, paranoia, insomnia (lack of sleep), helplessness, depression, and physical injury. Beyond the health costs, cyberstalking causes financial costs and the loss of friendships for victims, including their having to change or abandon phone numbers, addresses, hobbies, jobs, or schools.

Sexual harassment involves repetitive unwanted sexual solicitation, initiated conversations, or behaviors, including exposing one's genitalia. Cybersexual harassment is a form of cyber harassment that involves recurring unwanted digital sexual contact, including digital communication about sexual behaviors or the consensual sharing of sexually explicit images from the harasser. One enduring issue with cybersexual harassment is that it can be anonymous; therefore, it may be difficult to identify the harasser.

Research suggests that one in five teens between ages twelve and seventeen experience unwanted online exposure to sexually explicit material. In some states, cybersexual harassment is considered illegal. Teens are twice as likely to experience unwanted online sexual exposure (20%) than they are to experience online unwanted sexual solicitation, or people asking them to engage in sex (11%). Scholars such as Michele Ybarra, a researcher at Internet Solutions for Kids, Inc., found that victims of unwanted sexual solicitation demonstrated a greater degree of mental issues, including more frequent substance use. Compared to heterosexual and cisgender individuals, those who identify as gay, lesbian, bisexual, transgender, or gender fluid are more frequently victims of online sexual violence.

One of the risks of cybersexual harassment is that it can later become physical sexual assault or rape. Researchers from the CDC and the University of Southern California (USC) surveyed how frequently teens experienced and engaged in online bullying and sexual harassment from 2008 to 2013. They found traditional and cybersexual harassment as well as bullying tends to co-occur (occur at the same time) for teens. They also found students who felt more anger, had more pornographic exposure, and more positive attitudes toward traditional masculinity were more likely to engage in online harassment (i.e., harassing others). These students were less likely to feel supported by the people around them, and there was less parental awareness of what they were doing. But they felt a greater sense of school belonging and had more self-esteem. Teens who reported harassing other teens tended to be more popular at school and reported more positive or favorable self-views. Other studies find more alcohol consumption was related to engaging in cybersexual harassment and other forms of teen dating violence.

Revenge porn, cyberstalking, and cybersexual harassment all involve intrusive behaviors that repetitively interrupt, violate, and threaten the victim's life, creating a continuous emotional challenge that can be difficult to avoid and overcome. Therefore, they each can contribute to chronic and severe stress in victims, with long-lasting effects on psychological and relational health. For instance, these victims may find trusting future romantic partners difficult, and there may be additional challenges in developing relationships. The damaging impact on self-confidence can also endure far beyond the time when the person was being victimized.

11. How can social media use cause teen stress?

The amount of time and ways in which teens use social media can contribute to loneliness, diminished self-esteem, and family conflict. This is because social media usage often leads people to compare their lives with the images and messages that others have posted online. Moreover, teens' efforts to manage all their relationships via social media can become overwhelming and exhausting as well as a form distraction from other important goals, increasing teens' stress.

Social media, which includes social networking sites such as Facebook, Instagram, and Snapchat, has become increasingly popular among all ages, but it remains most popular among teenagers. In a 2019 study, the Pew Research Center found that 85 percent of U.S. teens use YouTube, 72 percent use Instagram, and another 69 percent use Snapchat. That same year, Common Sense Media found that 70 percent of teens report using social media multiple times a day. This percentage has doubled since 2014. Social media use seems to be growing increasingly common within the lives of teen. Yet, their feelings toward social media are mixed. Many teens feel it benefits their relationships with friends and family, their creative self-expression, and their self-esteem. However, the majority also agree that social media has exposed them to racist, sexist, or homophobic content as well as cyberbullying and harassment. They also acknowledge that they are being distracted from homework, friends, sleep, and meals.

Recently, teen social media use has raised concern among parents, educators, pediatricians, and psychologists, but scientists have found mixed results. Recent research by Jeanne Twenge, a professor of psychology at San Diego State University, has suggested that the general increase in mental health diagnoses among teenagers is related to the increase in technology use. Common Sense Media found that teens report feeling less lonely and depressed because of social media. Some researchers, such as Robert Tokunaga, a professor of communicology at the University of Hawai'i at Manoa, and Robert LaRose, a professor of media and information at Michigan State University, suggest that spending an excessive amount of time on social media is associated with loneliness, depression, and anxiety. Researchers currently believe this is because it is used as a coping tool and because social media can lead to arguments with parents as well as friends and compete with schoolwork.

Using social media to deal with emotions does not allow a person to reflect on the cause of their feelings, such as stress. The compulsion to use social media can distract from jobs, chores, time spent with friends or family, and homework, creating conflict within relationships. Tokunaga and LaRose also mention that people who use social media more frequently tend to be the people who are more lonely, depressed, or anxious in the first place. It is unclear yet which came first: the social media use or the loneliness, depression, or anxiety.

Other researchers find that the size of a teen's social network—the number of friends or followers they have—may explain some of the harm of social media. Nicole Ellison, a prominent researcher in the field of information science at Michigan University, speculates that this is because with more friends and followers, there may be more expectations of constant availability and a greater challenge created from the need to manage one's identity across groups of friends (e.g., friends from soccer club, friends from drama, cousins, and siblings). These challenges increase biological stress, which increases cortisol after waking in the morning and inflammation in the body, which may impact health.

Social media also appears more likely to produce stress when mainly used to learn about others' lives rather than to express creativity and share updates about one's own life. Psychologists and communication experts have found that people who tend to only "lurk" online are more likely to feel unhappy. Lurking involves passive viewing and reacting to other people's posts. People who lurk often scroll through posts and begin to feel that others have a more fulfilling life. This occurs through the process of social comparison, which is the act of contrasting one's personal experiences with others' experiences.

Although social comparison occurs without social media, people tend to manage their reputation and aim to selectively present themselves online. People often share what they think shows them in the most positive light. After spending hours exposed to these selective images of others, people tend to engage in what scholars call a "downward social comparison." When downward social comparisons occur, people evaluate their own life more negatively in comparison to those surrounding them. Downward social comparisons create dissatisfaction with life and challenges where there may be none, contributing to poorer mental health and greater stress.

In addition to the impact of social media content on teen stress, the time that it requires to remain connected and informed about their friends' lives can become excessive. This may be fueled by a concept called the fear of missing out (FOMO). Regardless of the motivation, social media can contribute to stress by replacing time that could be spent fully and deeply connecting with friends and family or engaging in homework, chores, or exercise. Spending time on social media can replace exercise or important in-person conversations and experiences. This ultimately interferes with teens' ability to cope with stress.

The time spent on social media may also cause stress because parents and teens fail to come to an agreement about appropriate social media uses. Parents may create rules to limit the internet but fail in enforcing or maintaining these rules with their teens and their own technology use. Social media can also lead to arguments when a parent or caregiver violates a teenager's privacy by viewing their real or fake accounts without permission or, worse, logging into the accounts to view them. Parents and teens can make agreements about a certain level of access to their teens' social media posts, follow each other on social media, or spend time on social media together to reduce the chances of this happening. Otherwise, these challenges at home may create chronic stress for the teen by disrupting their home life and reducing their perceived level of parental trust.

Although social media often contributes to stress, it can also alleviate stress. This depends on the teen's friends, family, and community; social media's impact on their identity; and the ways in which they use social media. If used as a channel for self-expression and connecting with people that the teen is close to, social media can be immensely beneficial and even helpful in preventing stress (see question 44 about positive digital coping).

12. How can the fear of missing out (FOMO) cause teen stress?

The anxiety experienced when a person feels they could have made a better decision or that others are living a more enjoyable or exciting life is known as the fear of missing out (FOMO). FOMO causes stress because it can lead a teen to feel less positively about themselves, excluded, or overwhelmed by all the information they need to have. These negative evaluations of a teen's life or lifestyle are harmful because they diminish the teen's satisfaction and self-esteem.

The fear of missing out has been categorized as a form of anxiety. It is commonly defined as the concern that others are having rewarding experiences from which a person is absent. FOMO is likely to occur to teenagers because they are in a developmental stage where they desire personal and social exploration; they want to understand their world and who they are within it. In this stage of identify formation, teens are more sensitive to the need to belong. They want to be likable and often aim to fit in. Therefore, they often want experiences or materials that help them solidify their identity and gain a place in their social world.

Although FOMO existed before smartphones and social media, it is more common now. FOMO is the perception of "not having or being included enough," which produces teen stress. It also generates teen stress by creating a pressure to be aware of the trends and viral news and videos that their friends or community may care about. To avoid FOMO, teenagers face the challenging task of constantly monitoring news, entertainment, and social media so as not to miss any chance to connect or engage with peers.

Sherry Turkle, a professor at MIT in the Department of Social Studies of Science and Technology, has studied teens' use of technology for over a decade. She argues that technology reduces time for self-reflection for teens, creating the "tethered self." The tethered self is always distracted from the present and expected be responsive and available all day long, seven days a week, with no exceptions. In her studies, teens have shared that although being tethered is a challenge and contributes to daily anxiety, they have found that it is not possible to maintain a friendship unless they are regularly available online. FOMO may cause stress because teenagers feel they have too much information to process and manage, but it can also cause stress when the anxiety of not checking their mobile devices becomes overwhelming. FOMO also poses challenges within daily life for teenagers because it can create distractions from the present moment.

The anxiety surrounding FOMO can contribute to self-criticism and negative self-beliefs both because teens feel less present and because they compare themselves to their friends and feel they are less attractive or have inferior lives. The damage to self-esteem may reinforce the lack of trust and concerns about relationships that reinforce or make FOMO stronger. As FOMO increases phone checking or device use, teens may frustrate friends and family, causing arguments and alienation. This combination then erodes the teenager's mental health, contributing to their experiences and symptoms of depression and anxiety.

Some scholars are concerned that FOMO can facilitate an addiction to and dependency on smartphones. The excessive use of or dependence on devices to connect with friends and remain informed may become problematic in other ways as well. FOMO is related to an experience of withdrawal and anxiety when people are incapable of accessing or using their smartphone or any internet-connected device. This condition is called *nomophobia*. Nomophobia—short for *no mobile phobia*—is the fear that arises from having a lack of access to one's mobile phone or mobile device. Nomophobia is classified as a form of social anxiety. It is experienced when enduring distance from or absence of one's personal phone creates concerns about the obstacle to potential relationships or communication (receiving or responding to messages). Nomophobia is explained such that the lack of access to mobile device may be perceived as a threat to social acceptance or belonging.

Nomophobia can become paralyzing and can pose challenges to academic performance and relational development. It can also cause withdrawal symptoms, like from a drug addiction, when separated from these devices. These damaging outcomes of nomophobia have become internationally acknowledged problems. Not all countries consider it a disorder to be diagnosed by a medical professional, but scholars have identified technology cleansing, such as visiting a detox camp where teens explore the outdoors, as a potential treatment. Other scientists suggest that mindfulness and meditation may be powerful methods for curing or diminishing nomophobia.

13. How can being online, using smartphones, and playing video games become addictive and cause teen stress?

Addictions to the internet, smartphones, and video games signal that teens' strategies for coping with stress and managing their moods and feelings have become reliant on these media. This dependency creates and increases teen stress because their uses of the internet, smartphones, and video games begin to interrupt important goals. Teenagers who have symptoms of addiction often experience more arguments with their friends and family. They may become more socially isolated and underperform at school or work, reducing the teens' self-esteem or confidence and creating stress. The challenge of changing teens' habits and breaking their dependency can also become a source of stress and often requires professional support.

Around the world, physicians and psychologists have begun to recognize and diagnose internet, smartphone, and video game addiction. The APA has recognized these addictions in the newest *Diagnostic and Statistical Manual for Mental Disorders (DSM-5)*. These addictions afflict less than 10 percent of the total population and less than 5 percent of teenagers in the United States. Enjoying the internet, smartphones, or video games frequently or for multiple hours is not necessarily harmful. The symptoms of addiction involve irritability, disregard of other tasks, and problems at school, work, and home.

Although addictions to the internet, smartphones, and video games involve different behaviors, research finds that they are all related to a lack of coping skills when faced with negative emotions. These behavioral addictions often slowly overwhelm other habits that are important for maintaining a healthy mind and body, such as eating regularly, sleeping enough hours, or having meaningful conversations with people. The more the dependency affects teens' health, creating more negative emotions and less clear thoughts, the more the teenagers may feel the urge and need to rely on their devices.

Social psychologist Douglas Gentile refers to the ironic effect of addiction as the downward spiral of addiction. The most harmful impacts of these behavioral addictions are often on teens' identity—the way they view their abilities to have friends and be successful at school or work. Teens' identity and long-term well-being, such as the success of their future career and mental health, are often harmed by the stigma or judgments of others about their addiction. Often, the harsh and critical judgments of friends and family, who may tell the teens, that they "just do not want to try" or they "are lazy," can lead these teenagers to isolate themselves. The teenagers' isolation can lead to loneliness. Over time, these teens begin to have a negative self-view or become less trusting of others, which increases their likelihood to remain addicted as well as their risk for depression and violence.

Teens who experience a dependency on these devices often have less emotional intelligence. These teens experience a greater challenge in describing their own emotions and identifying the emotions of others. Therefore, as compared to their peers, these teens are more likely to feel stressed when engaging with other people: friends, family, teachers, and schoolmates. These teenagers also experience more stress because they have trouble identifying their needs and expressing them to their family and friends. Due to their challenges with telling people when they need more support or when they want an apology, they are more frequently frustrated.

The impact of video game addiction on aggression and violence is still debated. Thus far, studies have found that although teens who play more violent video games are more at risk for aggression, the increased risk is weak or small. In other words, video game addiction could be a factor that contributes to aggression but is not a substantial contributor or cause. Rather, the findings from investigating thousands of individuals around the globe over the last five decades suggests that there are environmental factors, such as the violence and aggression teens see in their family, community, or among close friends, that have a larger impact. Video game addiction and the resulting exposure to violent content can exacerbate these issues. In other words, preventing or targeting the video game addiction may not cure the problem.

Diagnosing children on the autism spectrum with any of the above addictions is currently under research. Much of the definition of behavioral addiction and the research that led to the creation of it as a diagnosis was built off of neurotypical adults, or adults with a more typical brain structure. The psychiatric community has come to question whether these behaviors are equally harmful among children and teenagers in general. These researchers are exploring the effects of video games on different brain wiring. Scholars find there are advantages and disadvantages of being neurotypical or neuroatypical. Thus far, there is evidence that for neuroatypical teenagers, the behaviors that may be characterized as problematic, such as using devices to avoid large social gatherings, are actually soothing and beneficial.

14. How can multitasking cause teen stress?

Multitasking is a misunderstood concept. Teens' multitasking and that of their caregivers can contribute to teens' stress, as it interrupts their quality family time, time with friends, and schoolwork. *Multitasking* refers to engaging in multiple tasks at the same time, which involves mentally shifting attention between two or more tasks. Multitasking can be healthy when teens do it intentionally and with relevant tasks. Yet, it can cause stress when it becomes a reason for arguments between teens and their families, teachers, and friends; reduces their sense of connection with friends; or decreases their focus on school, hurting their grades.

In 2004, Common Sense Media conducted a survey of American teens and found that 81 percent of teens multitasked with multiple media devices at least once a week. In 2015, it repeated the study and revealed that children and adolescents switch between media on devices (e.g., smartphones and laptops) almost every ten seconds. In 2019, it found that 47 percent of all teens often listen to music, 24 percent often text, 19 percent often use social media, and 19 percent have the television on while doing their homework. Sixty percent of teens reported that they think multitasking helps them, and 34 percent thought it made no difference. Yet, of this, 6 percent of those who thought it was harmful said that the majority of them thought social media hurt their work while studying. But is multitasking harming teens more than they think?

Multitasking is a term that has created confusion and debate among scientists and nonscientists. Popular beliefs are that multitasking is a "myth" and always damaging, yet this is not supported by research. Multitasking was originally defined as the brain's processing (via listening, reading, viewing, or responding) of multiple tasks at the same time. Scientists once disagreed about whether the mind is capable of multitasking and now agree that people rapidly switch (within milliseconds) between tasks, creating the experience of processing two tasks at the same time. Each switch may have a cost to accuracy and efficiency (how quickly a task is completed), but this cost, or its harmfulness, depends on the difficulty of the tasks, the familiarity with tasks, and whether they require similar senses. Multitasking is possible because the body can engage in multiple tasks; for instance, most people have drunk water while walking, talked during a movie, taken notes on something heard, or danced to music.

Multitasking is easier when the tasks are relevant to another or support one another. Driving is a great example of this. For instance, a driver shifts between tasks that share one goal, such as checking the back mirror, watching the road, and signaling to change lanes. Similarly, taking notes while listening to a lecture can help teens to learn the material better because the two tasks are related. In these cases, switching between tasks has a small cost and is ultimately beneficial. The integration of information increases driving skills and knowledge about the course topic, respectively. People can become trained in multitasking and improve their ability to multitask as they get more familiar with tasks, such as checking the mirror and viewing the road ahead.

In juxtaposition, when multitasking with a difficult homework assignment, such as writing a book report or completing tough math problems, and another task, such as watching a new episode of a dramatic show, the cost of switching increases. This way of multitasking increases the challenge of completing and solving the problems accurately because the goal of watching television interrupts and competes with the goal of completing the homework. For instance, a funny or shocking moment in the show may interrupt the teen at a moment when they are understanding how to solve the problem. At this point, the teenager may choose to pause or turn off the TV to focus on the homework. The more frequent and longer the interruptions last, the harder the teen will need to work to remember where they had stopped working. Because the goals of watching the show for its plot and solving math problems are completely unrelated to one another, they are more disruptive to each other.

Research suggests that when teenagers acknowledge or plan for their homework to be the main goal and purposefully plan to use music, texting with a friend, a chat on social media, or television to help complete it, it is often less harmful and stressful. In other words, if teens plan to make and use media that feels relevant to their goals, it is less likely to be harmful. Similarly, distractions are less common when teens multitask with classical or familiar music in the background or a show they have watched many times and so are familiar with the plot. This is because the task of listening to music or watching the show is less difficult and unlikely to shock them. While teens, like adults, multitask to feel more productive, their multitasking differs from adults because teens often find their tasks more relevant to each other.

One challenge teens experience with multitasking homework and media is that it can lead to procrastination. Teens report that they may unintentionally focus on the show for a longer period of time. The avoidance or ignoring of an important goal is known as procrastination. Leonard Reinecke, a professor of communication in Johannes Gutenberg University Mainz, has found that the search for momentary relief can instead lead to procrastination. Entertaining content such as a television show or social media feed can lead to anxiety—a dreading feeling—about returning to the task of listening in class or completing homework. Thus, multitasking can lead to avoiding original goals or important tasks. Teens can experience this avoidance of other goals not only at school but also with friends and family.

Teens may find multitasking stressful because of its effect on their ability to listen in class and spend quality time with friends. Larry Rosen, a professor of psychology at California State University, Dominguez Hills, also found that multitasking with Facebook or texting during a lecture reduces how much information students retain. The irrelevant information teens see on social media interrupts their ability to retain class lectures. When this happens frequently at school and home, teens receive poorer grades. At this point, teenagers who are learning to reflect on their behaviors and plan their future may need guidance to reflect and come up with a strategy for how they will behave in school or at home. Rosen, PhD, has been working on developing interventions to teach teens mindfulness and better media and multitasking habits.

Teens report feeling annoyed and frustrated when their friends or parents multitask around them. Morgan Ames, a researcher at the School of Information at the University of California, Berkeley, conducted focus groups and interviews with teens to learn more about the ways multitasking and relationships are related. In her research, teens shared that they feel less important when their friends check their phones regularly or ignore them to use their phone. Teens felt stressed by their own multitasking, which was caused by a constant need to be present to friends both online and in person. Teens report that multitasking can also lead to an overwhelming amount of information or communication to manage and exhaustion from their relationships, known as information or communication overload.

15. How can academic pressure cause teen stress?

While education and the pursuit of a fulfilling or well-paying job or career can benefit a teenager long term, the challenge of achieving good grades can be overwhelming. Academic pressure, or the expectation to complete and succeed in coursework at school, can create stress. Teenagers often find obstacles to their self-esteem in their academic performance, and they experience arguments with their parents. Teenagers can also feel fearful, fatigued, and overwhelmed because of the uncertainty around or expected effect of academics on their future.

According to a 2019 study by the Pew Research Center, teenagers say academics are their top source of stress; 61 percent of teens say they feel *a lot* of pressure to get good grades. In its research, Pew found that boys and girls as well as teenagers of various income households are equally likely to feel pressure to get good grades. Teens report that it feels as though their entire life depends on their academic success. Academic stress is universal, but is it benefiting or harming teens?

Studies on scholarship from Stanford University have found that academic expectations for teens often help them build their confidence. In other words, teens who have adults, siblings, or mentors who believe that they can succeed and teach them how to succeed at school perform better on exams and book reports. Parents and caregivers can educate their teenagers on how to learn and perform well at school. Successful communication is focused on guiding teenagers in achieving their goals and providing support to help manage their stress from studying for an exam or reading a book.

Contrastingly, teenagers who perceive messages of shame or pressure to achieve are less likely to perform well. Research finds that, on average, teens who feel parents shame and force them or are anxious about their studying habits or grades are less likely to put effort into their education. When caregivers or family members criticize or judge a teenager for performing below expectations, they can reduce the teen's motivation to put effort into academics and increase their stress. The disappointment or labels of "lazy" or "stupid" by parents or family members lead teens to negative self-concepts or views of themselves. This lower self-concept as well as frequent stress about school over time results in teens having less energy to pursue their schoolwork.

Academic pressure or the expectations for a teenager to perform well academically can lead to perfectionism, which is an unhealthy behavior in which the teen obsesses over meeting excessively high standards. Perfectionism has been associated with mental illness, especially depression and anxiety. Over time, the self-critical and self-judgmental ways perfectionist teenagers speak to themselves lead to less self-care, such as not getting enough sleep. Teens who sleep less can feel foggy or unclear in the way they think; they tend to have more negative moods and views of themselves. This sensation of feeling unable to think, focus, or accomplish their school-related goals can result in dropping out as well as suicidal ideation or having thoughts about self-injury and death.

Previous research suggests that academic pressure is not only associated with the exhaustion of energy to engage in schoolwork but also problematic media use and internet addiction. Teenagers may not have support from their family, friends, or teachers for finding solutions to their academic stress. In these situations, teens may cope with their feeling of being overwhelmed by engaging in social media or video games. Fernando Andrade, PhD, from the School of Social Work at the University of Michigan, found that the pressure for positive academic performance (such as getting As) was associated with substance use, such as alcohol, tobacco, or marijuana. This academic pressure can be more intense for athletes because they need to perform well physically and academically. In these cases, their exhaustion or lack of sleep can impact both their potential for a career in their sport as well as their grades. It may also be dangerous for their health and lead them to use substances such as energy drinks and alcohol to cope with their stress.

Academic stress can also be a direct outcome of the lack of resources that they have to cope with the schoolwork. Therefore, researchers have found that teenagers from poorer or less educated families tend to experience more learning burnout—the mental or emotional exhaustion from learning. The poor grades they receive despite their efforts increase their stress and lead to feelings that they cannot cope with academic challenges, resulting in exhaustion. Yet, teenagers who feel a closeness with their families and experience less conflict or arguments are able to overcome these challenges.

Academic pressure can harm teenagers' abilities to succeed in their coursework and obtain a high grade point average (GPA), which affects their likelihood to get into college or graduate. Yet, potential unhealthy habits (such as diminished sleep), harm to self-esteem, and depression are of greater concern. Supporting teenagers in planning for academic success and encouraging them to achieve their goals can help manage the stress and improve their grades at school.

16. How does the process of being college-bound and beginning college create teen stress?

According to NCES, about 70 percent of recent high school graduates were enrolled in colleges or universities in 2018. While this statistic itself is impressive, it is missing the many who aspired to attend college but were unable to for a variety of reasons. If nothing else, this statistic demonstrates that the majority of adolescents who complete their high school degree aim for college.

Moreover, a number of external pressures (schools, parents, peers, and nonprofit organizations) have led students at increasingly younger ages to worry about college. Thus, high schoolers have begun to experience concern about (1) the necessity of a degree for even the most menial job, (2) the expensive nature (high costs) of college, and (3) the growing expectations of high schools, colleges, and universities. Because these demands have become commonplace, teens and adults may struggle to understand why these challenges are extremely difficult for teens. The answer is related to the teenagers' cognitive (brain and mind) development.

Teenagers' brains change to have greater planning capacities, but their hormonal changes from puberty often have unintended consequences, including greater impulsivity. College planning requires careful effort. Teens must choose schools, learn the requirements of schools, and create and accomplish goals that meet those requirements. The journey to the college or university of one's dreams includes enrolling in the required courses, ensuring courses are taken in a timely fashion, knowing the GPA calculations for each school, obtaining the necessary scores on the standardized tests (though these may be removed), participating in enough extracurricular activities (sports, clubs, and community service), and earning or finding enough money to apply. This is an enormous project. For most teens, it is the biggest project they have ever undertaken. The amount of forward thinking, planning, and delayed gratification it demands can become overwhelming for teens' developing abilities to evaluate long-term consequences.

Although time management is an important skill to learn and college can be a worthwhile challenge, teens can struggle to manage their time. Teens are often under the guidance of their parents, but they still have to balance and prioritize their own academic, social, and personal goals. Between the pressures of college and finding their identity, teens' academic and social goals often outweigh their self-care needs or come at the expense of their physical health. In other words, they choose to spend their energy and time on homework, making swim meets or theater practice, and keeping up with friends instead of sleeping enough and eating well.

In 2019, the Pew Research Center reported that around 20 percent of teens feel similarly pressured to be involved in extracurricular activities. Unhealthy outcomes of this strain on their time and bodies are often related to sleep. Research dictates that adolescents (teenagers) require eight to ten hours of sleep for healthy development, but to accomplish their myriad goals, they often abandon sleep. The National Sleep Foundation reported that nearly 66 percent of high school students reported getting fewer than eight hours of sleep, and one study even found that only 15 percent reported sleeping eight and a half hours on school nights. This decrease in sleep is related to an increased risk of obesity, problems with focus and memory, and even lower emotional intelligence, which is the ability to recognize and respond to emotions.

The teenage years are an important time for creating coping strategies for emotions. These skills are necessary for navigating the successes and failures that come with transitioning into adulthood. Marked with the emotional challenges of first romances, first jobs, and the first years of driving, the reduced sleep and sleep quality can have serious consequences for adolescents. Their reduced sleep may interfere with their ability to focus and increase the intensity of their emotional experiences. Thus, teens' lack of sleep can also lead to a series of risky decisions.

College-related stress not only threatens healthy sleep; it can also lead to unhealthy habits, such as the use of unprescribed medications such as Adderall and Ritalin to aid studying. These medications are usually prescribed for ADHD and ADD, but they are abused by students to aid or extend their focus for longer hours. Students may also engage in habits that are indirectly damaging to maintain their attention. Research has found that these often include ingesting large amounts of caffeine, undereating, overeating, or eating unhealthy foods that are high in sugar and fat. These in turn further exhaust their minds and bodies, ultimately contributing to burnout.

17. How can friendships and peer pressure cause teen stress?

In the teenage years especially, friends can be both a source of stress and a source of support. Choosing and managing friends and friendships can be difficult for teenagers. Teenagers may struggle to find friends who support them, encourage their identity development, and help build their self-esteem (i.e., confidence). Teens' friends can create stress by being harsh or critical, regularly creating arguments and drama, and hurting teens' sense of trust. Their friends may also cause stress by pressuring them to engage in risky and unsafe behaviors.

In 2019, the Pew Research Center found that 29 percent of teenagers experience a lot of pressure to look good, and 37 percent feel some pressure to look good. Forty-seven percent of teens reported feeling at least a little pressure to be sexually active, 35 percent reported feeling at least a little pressure to drink alcohol, and 34 percent reported feeling at least a little pressure to use drugs. When they described their relationships, 62 percent reported experiencing people who "put them down," and 29 percent reported that they wished they had more good friends. In 2018, the health insurer Cigna conducted a national survey and found that loneliness has become increasingly prevalent, especially among youth. In 2020, Cigna found that 79 percent of eighteen to twenty-two-year-old Americans reported feeling lonely as compared to 50 percent of Americans aged fifty-two to seventy-one years old.

The challenges of making and managing relationships with friends can leave teens feeling lonely. Researchers at Brigham Young University have found that the stress of loneliness decreases teens' mental and physical health. These researchers have argued that loneliness can be more detrimental to health than obesity or smoking cigarettes. Good friendships can protect teens from suicide, anxiety, depression, and stress and increase mental well-being, self-esteem, and optimism. Meanwhile, loneliness and experiences of social isolation may impact teens' sense of friendship self-efficacy or their confidence to engage and communicate with friends, resolve arguments, and manage emotions. Teens with few close friends are more likely to be the victims of cyberbullying and bullying as well as peer pressure.

Similar to loneliness, teen friendships that involve more frequent arguments, drama, and secrecy also create stress. These forms of friend-related stress have been found to increase the risk for social isolation, lower self-esteem (i.e., a less positive views of oneself), and less involvement with friends. These teens are also less likely to engage with friends at and after school. Yet, they are more likely to engage in risky behavior, such as drug and alcohol use. Stress caused by other teenagers, even those who are not necessarily their friends, have been associated with symptoms of anxiety and depression. Research has revealed that girls who experience more friend- or peer-related stress are more likely to have poor mental health.

Moreover, friends can cause or increase each other's stress by being critical, harsh, or engaging in co-ruminating. Co-brooding is the act of reviewing and repeating negative experiences, thoughts, and feelings with friends. This may include competing for who has it worse with phrases such as, "I'm so stupid; I failed that test and I'm never going to college, have fun without me," or "That's the worst your social life is over." When friends co-brood, they engage in catastrophizing. Catastrophizing is a cognitive distortion in which a person assumes one negative experience is indicative of something much worse and jumps to the conclusion that they are experiencing or will experience a disaster. When friends co-brood, they often do not offer validation (listening and understanding each other) and support; instead, they focus on how a situation has become overwhelmingly terrible. By catastrophizing and repeating the situation, friends make a problem feel more challenging. Research finds these friends are more likely to experience depressive symptoms.

Due to pubescent changes to their minds and bodies, teenagers have more influence on each other's choices and emotions. Teens often seek to be liked by other teens, which can lead them to engage in helpful behaviors, such as studying, or unhelpful behaviors, such as alcohol abuse. Peer pressure, which usually includes unhealthy behaviors, may be a source of stress. Peer pressure occurs when a friend or any other teenager repeatedly encourages or tells a teenager to do something, even if they do not want to do it. Teens usually feel a need to conform or act more similarly to their friends and peers to fit in.

Social media can also create a less obvious form of peer pressure via the images people post of what is likeable. Research has found that teenagers are likely to conform to popular teenagers' behaviors. For instance, one study found that teenagers who thought that popular teenagers engage in sexting, sending sexual messages over text, were ten times more likely to also sext. Teens' friends and peers also influence each other's body image, or how they perceive their bodies. The images found on social media also create a standard for what is considered "normal" or "attractive," such as being thin or having defined abs, which increases teenagers' stress and lowers their self-esteem.

Peer pressure can also involve other risky behaviors. Substance use, including prescribed medications, marijuana, and alcohol, among friends is one of the best predictors of whether teenagers also use substances. Teens have also reported that having a friend or other teenager in the car can impact their likelihood to drive more erratically (less safe), experience or perpetrate sexual harassment, or behave aggressively. In Penn State's Promoting School-community-university Partnerships to Enhance Resilience (PROSPER) survey of high school students, teenagers with friends who engage in self-harm were more likely to engage in self-harm as well. Not only is the pressure from their friends stressful but teenagers also experience stress as an outcome of their risky behaviors.

Teenagers can be resilient to the peer pressure and friend- or peer-related stress if they feel they receive support elsewhere. Studies show that teenagers who felt little support from their school, such as their friends or the staff members and teachers, or their families were more likely to be influenced or affected by peer pressure. Teenagers with more support were more resilient to these stressors. Therefore, studies find they experience fewer depressive symptoms.

18. How do romantic relationships cause teen stress?

Puberty, which on average begins at ten years old, causes physical changes and leads teenagers to begin seeking romantic relationships. The goal of having a romantic relationship brings many new challenges. Romance can also be confused by the hormonal changes driving increased sexual interest and teens' exploration of what is attractive. Teen romantic relationships are also harder to define, more unstable, and likely to involve more arguments. During the teenage years, dating violence, jealousy, and cheating are more common due to teens' impulsivity and emotional intensity, though still harmful. These negative romantic experiences have greater impacts on stress because of teens' sensitivity to relationships. Finally, teenagers may and are more likely to experience intimate partner violence, which can be traumatic and cause them to feel shame.

Although dating is very common among teenagers, Child Trends shared findings from *Monitoring the Future: A Continuing Study of American Youth (1976–2017)* in which teenagers reported less dating than ever before. In 2015, Pew Research Center found that 35 percent of teens have some experience dating. Its study found that the likelihood to engage in dating increases significantly among older teens as compared to younger teens. Teens reported that the majority of their conversations with people they are dating or interested in dating occur through social media or via texting. They report this helps them feel closer to one other. The expectation of being available and potential information found on social media contributed to teens' stress. In 2018, the Centers of Disease Control and Prevention (CDC) found that 26 percent of women and 15 percent of men experience intimate partner violence (either physical, sexual, psychological aggression, or stalking) before age eighteen. These statistics are higher among sexual minorities.

Previous scientific findings suggest that the impact of romantic relationships on teen stress is driven by the consequence for identity development. Due to teenagers' aims to understand themselves, the perceived success and ability to create romantic relationships becomes more important. Being able to create a stable and health romantic relationship is foundational for teenagers' ability to grow emotionally independent from their parents. Yet, as teenagers develop their own identities, they become more capable and more likely to engage in intimacy and healthy relationship development. However, this process causes stress because of the novelty of these experiences. Teenagers must learn how to deal with challenges in romantic relationships and in determining whom to trust for support.

Maintaining and developing relationships is also a challenge for teenagers because they have less emotional stability and more intense emotions than adults or children. Specifically, the ability to communicate twenty-four hours a day and seven days a week across many platforms has introduced new challenges for teenagers and their romantic relationships. Twenty-seven percent of American teenagers report that social media has led to feelings of jealousy or uncertainty about their relationships and that breaking up with a text message, which is the least acceptable to them, is still rather common. Ten percent report having impersonated their previous romantic partner, 8 percent have sent embarrassing photos of their ex to someone else, and 4 percent have used GPS to track them without their knowledge. These behaviors are violating someone else's privacy.

Teens also report harassing, monitoring, and controlling the people they are dating or are sexually involved with over technology, which are examples of violent dating behaviors. These result in a great deal of stress. The consequences of stalking, physical violence, and psychological violence among teenagers include increased symptoms of depression; increased use of tobacco, drugs, or alcohol; and more lying, theft, bullying, violence, and thoughts about suicide or self-harm. This is because dating violence can influence teenagers' fear, self-views, anger, and experiences of sadness. Teenagers' consequent violence and substance use are often unhealthy coping tools.

Studies have found that the quality of the teen-parent relationship predicts the likelihood of experiencing these forms of romance-related stress. Teenagers with a healthy sense of trust and self-esteem due to a trusting and loving relationship with their parents are more likely to seek help and find resources that can stop or prevent dating violence. The beliefs of teenagers' friends and their ability to validate or acknowledge the occurrence of dating violence are also predictors of prevention and healthy coping. The CDC recommends involving adults to find resources to educate teens about healthy technology communication.

The pursuit of romantic relationships can also create stress and pressure about one's sexual identity and willingness to engage in sexual activities. Teenagers who seek peer (fellow teenagers') approval are often unaware or uncomfortable with engaging in safe sexual practices. They may feel uncomfortable talking to their potential sexual partners about whether they have been tested for sexually transmitted diseases (STDs) or about using protection or birth control. The CDC finds that one in every four, or 25 percent, of sexually active teenagers has an STD. As compared to adults, sexually active teenagers are at a higher risk for getting an STD. The choice to engage in sexual activities and then the concerns about protecting each other's intimacy, health, and privacy cause of a great deal of stress.

Finally, teenagers may be faced with peer pressure, or the experience of feeling that others are trying to convince them to engage in behaviors. This pressure leads to impulsive behaviors and confusion that result in stressful emotions, such as regret and shame, after sexual and romantic interactions. This is especially challenging for teens given the permanent and uncontrollable uses of digital images and texts. However, studies show that having a positive parent-teen relationship and being surrounded by friends who are sexually responsible in their relationships increase teenagers' likelihood to also be sexually responsible.

19. How do teens' developing sexuality and sexual identity contribute to teen stress?

Driven by puberty, teens are becoming aware of sexual attraction to others as well as others' sexual attraction to them. Unique concerns and challenges about their identity as related to their birth-defined sex or sexual organs (such as a penis or vagina), sexual interest, and romantic partners bloom in these years. Teenagers can feel a great deal of confusion about their sexual interest without proper education from the adults around them to normalize the changes to their bodies and minds. This confusion, in addition to the potential bullying they experience as a result of their exploration, explains most of the stress they experience because of their sexuality.

In the teen years, the onset of puberty occurs as teens experience hormonal changes in their estrogen or testosterone levels. The adrenal gland's development has been demonstrated to create greater sexual interest and awareness. Previous research suggests these changes drive young people to spend increasingly more time with romantic partners than friends. While reveals itself in teenage years, the progression from recognizing to whom one is attracted to engaging in romantic or sexual behavior as well as identifying with one's sexuality does not necessarily occur within the same time frame or in the same order for everyone. Thus, exploring sexuality and romance and then ultimately identifying as heterosexual, lesbian, gay, bisexual, heteroflexible, or pansexual do not develop or become apparent at the same time or unfold in the same way for all youth. For some, it takes well into adulthood for others it's clear in their childhood. Regardless of sexuality, early romantic relationships involve challenges that increase daily stress levels.

There are strong social and cultural components to the timing of teenagers' dating (i.e., early or late teen years) and dating behaviors. For instance, teens who come from cultures in which the norm is not to date until adulthood may be less likely to date in early adolescence. On the other hand, researchers have found that in cultures that condemn early romantic and sexual engagement, early adolescents are more likely to keep their romantic interests a secret. Hidden sexual engagement between two heterosexual teens (i.e., those attracted to, romantic with, or sexually engaged with the opposite-sex) or gay, lesbian, or bisexual teens is stressful. Additionally research reveals that teens in secret sexual or romantic relationships are at a greater risk for violence.

The impact of hiding sexual interest and romantic partners on health includes its affects on teenagers' self-esteem. Teenagers aim to accomplish the important goal of solidifying their identity, or who they are. Teens who are told not to express emotions about their sexuality experience more shame and humiliation around their sexuality, which harms their health. This stress can decrease the chance for teenagers to find or talk to supportive and healthy romantic partners. It can diminish their likelihood to trust or feel lovable to their romantic partners. These teens have fewer people who can help them cope with their stress, weakening their mental health and leaving them vulnerable to risky ways of dealing with their stress, such as denial, violence, and substance use (using drugs or drinking). When compared to teenagers who recognize that their sexuality is a healthy aspect of their development, teens who experience shame surrounding their sexuality are disadvantaged.

The intersection of sexual experiences and romantic relationships is of critical importance for healthy adult relationships. During the teenage years, engaging in heavy sexual behaviors within a romantic relationship (i.e., with a boyfriend or girlfriend) has no relationship with depression, violence, substance abuse, or poor academic performance. Yet, teens experience more depression, violence, substance abuse, and poorer grades when they frequently engage in sexual behaviors outside of romantic relationships. An intimate relationship with a sexual partner increases the chance that sexual behaviors are not used to deal with stress. It can also decrease the chance (though the probability is not entirely removed) that the sexual partner will be violent.

Teens who have parent-child trust and experience positive relationships with their parents are more likely to engage in sexual behaviors in romantic relationships. Supportive relationships with parents or caregivers can significantly reduce the stress about sexual development, sexual interest, and sexual behaviors. Although parents and teens frequently avoid and feel uncomfortable discussing sex, researchers have found that open, understanding, and trust-creating discussions reduce sexual risk— even when parents and teenagers have differing opinions. These conversations often delay sexual behaviors and intercourse and increase safe-sex practices, such as using condoms and birth control, as well as discussions about sexual histories and testing with sexual partners.

These conversations between parents and teens are especially important because teenagers are also exposed to unrealistic representations of sexual encounters and romantic relationships via film, music, and television shows. The media is not only unrealistic about bodies but also sexual behaviors. This includes the underrepresentation of sexual minorities in television, music, and film (although recent statistics reveal this may be changing), which may lead teens to feel embarrassment or shame and thus cause stress. The challenges of teens' exploring their sexuality is often made more difficulty by the stigma and fear of isolation if they do not act like everyone they know, or what their friends and family define as "normal." This fear can sometimes be confirmed by their family's or friends' reactions to their sexual or gender-identity exploration. LGBTQ youth are more likely to experience more stress because they experience more bullying and social exclusion.

Teens of minority sexual and gender identities have been stated to have poorer mental health than their cisgender (those who identify with the gender that aligns with their assigned sex at birth) and heterosexual counterparts. Stephen Russell, PhD, and Jessica Fish, PhD, researchers in the Department of Human Development and Family Sciences at the University of Texas, Austin, summarized studies about mental health issues among lesbian, gay, bisexual, and transgender (LGBTQ) youth. They found more frequent depression and mood disorders, anxiety, PTSD, abuse of alcohol and other drugs, and suicidality for teens of sexual minorities. Suicide attempts are especially more common among male sexual minorities. Lesbians and bisexual female teenagers are more likely to exhibit problems with alcohol and drugs.

These sexual differences extend beyond attraction. As puberty highlights gender among teens, there are stressors about conforming to gender role standards or ideals. This stress can feel overwhelming because of teens' newly developed capacity for perspective-taking and the development of their identity. In 2018, Dennis Reidy and colleagues, from the Centers of Disease Control and Prevention (CDC), found evidence for the harmful stress teens feel about gender roles. The stress of not being seen as "manly," or masculine, enough is known as the *masculine discrepancy stress* (MDS). Reidy concluded that males who feel more MDS were lonelier, reported more emotional health issues, and engaged in more substance use.

However, Reidy found that it is not the feeling of being different from one's gender that is harmful. Rather, findings suggested that the bullying or exclusion, punishment, and overall victimization due to a teen male's discrepancy from his gender roles are greater contributors to poorer mental health and coping skills. Reidy found similar results for feminine discrepancy. However, for female adolescents, their lack of gender conformity was associated with trauma, and this trauma was the root of stress and poorer health. This work highlights the social challenges that teen males and females experience in differing from gender norms.

Nonetheless, the development of a sexual interest creates stressors by requiring young people to explore new feelings and engage in new types of relationships. The exploration of sexuality and romance is complicated by social judgment about sexuality and gender roles. Research supports that developing a healthy view of sex and romance is essential for long-term well-being. For sexual minorities and all teenagers, the access to social support—loved ones who can help solve problems and allow teens to express and feel validated in their emotions—creates healthier coping skills and increases the chances they will be well-adapted adults with healthy sexual and romantic lives.

20. How do teens experience financial stress?

Many teenagers experience financial stress or stress about money because they are hungry, unable to pay for college, fear for the well-being of family members, or dislike the arguments it causes among family members. However, more frequently, teenagers also begin to feel less supported by their family. In 2013 national study of teenagers by the APA, 65 percent reported that they were concerned about their family finances, which made it the third most commonly reported source of stress. Teenagers' insecurities about their family's financial situation are coupled with less control over the solution. Teenagers are limited in their ability to improve their family income.

Teenagers often experience financial stress because they see and hear conflicts or arguments between their parents or caregivers about money. They may experience conflicts or arguments with their parents, as the stress about money impacts the way their parents communicate or talk to them. Meanwhile, teens are only beginning to gain the capabilities of perspective-taking, or thinking about others' life experiences; planning; and considering consequences. These abilities allow them to be empathetic to or feel worried about their parents. Thus, teens who face poverty feel more stress and are more likely to experience poor mental health.

Rand Conger, a professor in human development and family studies at the University of California, Davis, and Glen Elder, a professor in sociology at the University of North Carolina–Chapel Hill, found that poverty increased the risk for marital instability and led parents to be more harsh, inconsistent, or uninvolved with their teens. While financial stressors are only part of the chaos that impacts family functions for teens, the increase in parental conflict (i.e., fights) can lead to less secure attachments, a lesser sense of safety, less trust in parents, and less self-confidence. These experiences may result in reduced social skills, poorer academic performance (i.e., lower grades), symptoms of depression or anxiety, and aggressive behavior. Financial stress extends beyond the threat to physical well-being.

Most research has found that money-related stress is also an outcome of the lack of joint family time. Studies have found that in financially challenged families, spending quality time and engaging in activities together can help teenagers experience less stress and more resilience. Teens benefit from the affection and the care and interest in their lives that their families show when interacting, especially during intentional family time. Family time can include sharing one good moment and bad moment from the day, eating together, or watching a television show together. Some studies find that losses in emotional security caused by financial insecurity can be a greater cause of stress than the financial insecurity alone. Emotional security is the feeling that they can depend on their family to care, love, and validate them.

The other path to stress for teenagers is the lack of control they have over the situation. Teenagers can feel their parents' stress, anxiety, or depression over money. Their family's financial troubles can be highly stressful to them because they are afraid of the increased challenges they might experience outside of their homes. Research has revealed that teenagers feel embarrassed about the clothes they wear to school and lack of school supplies, the fact that they cannot ask their parents for help, and the appearance of their parents. They also tend to feel afraid about their ability to find a job in their future and their ability to find a romantic partner who will be financially stable as an adult. The impact of teens' financial stress can often extend into adulthood.

Existing research suggests that while teens' mothers feel more stress, it is often the financial stress of fathers that impacts parenting and the way that parents treat their teens. This may be because fathers are assumed to play the role of breadwinners, such that they work to provide money and take care of their family. However, in situations in which fathers are unemployed or under financial stress, this can be challenging for the family. This pressure on fathers impacts the quality of their relationship with teens. These poorer relationships can create stress for the teenager.

Teens born into poverty or poor families are also more likely to be exposed to pollution from nearby traffic or industries, which can result in health problems. This includes greater likelihood for asthma. The noisiness of low-income homes may lead these teens to receive less sleep and food, creating challenges and making it more difficult to learn at school. They may experience less positive communication with the people around them, including fewer pleasant chats with the people that live in their neighborhood, and become exposed to violence. Family stress has been associated with addiction to alcohol or drugs, dropping out of school, and increased blood pressure or other heart problems.

Teens are sensitive to the impact of financial stress on their family due to their growth in empathy and because they are more likely to experience harsher parenting. They may struggle to focus in school or engage in unhealthy coping behaviors due to their frustrations about being unable to control the stressors. Teenagers who receive affection, including expressions of love and hugs, and engage in shared activities with their family experience fewer impacts from stress.

21. How can being a first-generation American create teen stress?

The youth who immigrate to or who are the first of their family to be born in the United States can experience unique burdens. They are often challenged by their need to assimilate to the American culture and yet often want to maintain the tradition of their previous or parents' culture. Thus, these teenagers have more challenges in defining their identity or in establishing their freedom. First-generation American teens may have also experienced traumas or financial stressors based on their family's immigration. They may also be victims of more discrimination and bullying at schools, increasing their challenges.

The 2010 U.S. Census found that there were approximately three million immigrant youth in the United States. Yet, children of immigrants represent one in four children in the United States, according to Child Trends. Recent research has found that Asian and Latinx immigrants represent the majority of the children of immigrants. Youth immigration has reached record highs globally, according to the United Nations High Commissioner for Refugees (UNHCR) in 2016. The Organisation for Economic Co-Operation and Development's (OECD) 2016 report of thirty-five countries, including the United States, revealed that immigrant children are met with aggression, anti-immigrant attitudes, and harsh political climates.

First-generation or immigrant teenagers can experience distinct adversities. In addition to coping with the developmental goals of their life stage, they are faced with learning how to adapt (e.g., learn English) and assimilate (i.e., fit in) within a new and perhaps unknown culture. Carola Suárez-Orozco, PhD, from the Human Development & Psychology department at UCLA, studies resilience development among immigrant youth. She and her colleagues found that immigrant youth can often feel like they are constantly living within two cultures. Compared to nonimmigrant-origin peers, they often have to engage in switching between cultural rules, identities, and languages, which is known as *code-switching*.

First-generation Americans not only engage in their own adaptation to the United States but also they support that of their parents or caregivers. They can become their parents' or siblings' language and cultural brokers. Stated differently, they need to serve as a translator who explains culture and exchanges the language for their families. Because of this role they play, they can become exposed to contexts often reserved for adulthood, such as taxes and speaking to health professionals on behalf of their parents. Some studies have indicated that over 90 percent of immigrant youths translate for parents, and this starts at young ages (eight or nine years). The need to broker language can be a source of stress for teenagers and may lead to feelings of discomfort, embarrassment, and even guilt. In the teen years, this is especially challenging as they aim to develop their independence.

Upon arriving in the United States, the resources available to immigrant teenagers can vary greatly. Scholars have found that immigrants tend to fall into the extremes of the highest and lowest economic segments. Due to the diversity in situations that lead to migration (by choice or by force), families may settle into privileged or poor neighborhoods. In immigrant-dense neighborhoods, these teens may be exposed to greater violence and instability as well as xenophobia, the fear of foreigners. Immigrant teens' experiences also vary between those that are non-European or people of color. Research has found that non-Europeans are more likely to be viewed as foreigners (non-Americans) even after assimilating to the American culture.

Research finds that discrimination is one of the main stressors among ethnic minorities and immigrant families. First-generation Americans experience more bullying and greater aggression than third-generation Americans or natives. Mexican-born teens in the United States often experience language hassles, such as people speaking negatively about their heritage language. This includes being criticized or bullied for speaking Spanish or for speaking English poorly. This bullying is associated with increased suffering from depression or other mental health issues. However, research has found that first-generation Americans who have close relationships with their family often experience a positive ethnic identity. These close family relationships protect teenagers from depression and other mental health issues.

In addition to these daily obstacles that immigrant teens have to overcome after moving to their new home country, they can experience traumas in the process of being undocumented, unaccompanied, or refugee children. Therefore, those who left their original country in the midst of war, violence, or natural disaster often have an elevated risk for depression and anxiety. Researchers believe this is an outcome of the frequent stress teens experienced in childhood that resulted in PTSD.

The ways that immigrant parents socialize their children have an impact on their consequent stress and mental health. For instance, scholars have found that cultural socialization for Mexican Americans, including discussions about their parents' experiences with discrimination, can help protect their self-esteem and reduce their chances of being socially withdrawn, aggressive, or engaged in substance abuse. Teens who have positive ethnic identities—who feel better about their unique cultural blend—engage in fewer risky behaviors and have better health. Bilingualism, the ability to speak two languages, has been evidenced as one way to increase positive ethnic identity and protect mental health.

22. How does body image create teen stress?

Teenagers' body image can create a great strain in their lives because of their developing identity, body, and sexuality. Teens experience dramatic physical changes and are psychologically sensitive to others' perceptions of them. Therefore, when teens view their physical appearance as unattractive or undesirable, it can cause distress. This stress can be initiated or created by parental pressures and exacerbated or worsened by trauma. If it becomes severe, the problem can become overwhelming and psychologically unhealthy.

Body image involves the thoughts and feelings that people have about their own appearances. This includes the way a teen may imagine their appearance and the way they perceive their image in the mirror. Body image becomes a focal point during the teenage years due to puberty. Hormones released from the adrenal cortex, such as estrogen and testosterone, create physical changes and are associated with the onset of romantic and sexual attraction. Sometimes this occurs as early as ten years old. These hormones facilitate the brain's development of a sensitivity to facial cues for sexual interest. Thus, teens begin to be concerned about who is expressing romantic interest to whom. They begin to understand and use concepts such as flirting.

This sensitivity to sexual interest can facilitate a greater awareness of the expectations for an attractive person and lead to negative social comparisons. The desire to be considered attractive and the pressure to conform to ideal body shape standards can contribute to poor body image or body dissatisfaction. Poor body image diminishes self-esteem and can even become so important to the teen that it overshadows other attitudes toward oneself.

Poor body image can also become self-reinforcing, as teens may believe that social failures or other negative experiences are related to their less than attractive body. For these reasons, diminished body image can lead to teens wanting to reassert control over their lives via unhealthy habits, such as dieting, binging, or fasting. The obsession with obtaining this ideal body increases the likelihood of mental health issues such as depression and eating disorders, including anorexia, bulimia, and obesity.

Researchers such as Kristen Harrison, PhD, a communication scholar at the University of Michigan, have found that poor body image is related to the types of people teens see in the media. Ideals of attractiveness, such as thinness, muscularity in men, and the small waists and large curves of the female body, are frequently portrayed in the media. These "ideal" body shapes often create unreasonable standards. Social cognitive theory, also known as social learning theory, developed by Albert Bandura, explains that children learn from what they see in the media. The theory argues models and actresses and actors teach children and teens about the types of behaviors and characteristics that will be rewarded. The theory explains that if the majority of the characters, celebrities, and public figures who achieve successful careers or find love are thin or muscular, then teens learn that they too must be thin or muscular to achieve success and "find love."

Similarly, cultivation theory, originally proposed by George Gerbner, suggests that cultural perspectives are developed via consistent exposure to the same stereotypes in media. Both social cognitive theory and cultivation theory research have revealed that consuming such media as television and video games can manifest in body dissatisfaction. Researchers argue that this is because of the skewed representations of women and men in popular media. Over time, media can not only affect body ideals but also the internalization (or acceptance) of gender stereotypes, including the hypersexualizing of women and machoism of men.

The use of digital tools to adjust the physical features of actresses make it such that the goals that teenagers set for attractiveness are unattainable. Filtered and manipulated images on social media contribute to increases in teens' body issues and diminish their self-esteem. Research finds that social media has the strongest effect on girls who tend to engage in social comparison. Social comparison is the act of comparing oneself to others. The unrealistic images online can lead teens to evaluate their own bodies more negatively. It is useful for teenagers to be aware of the degree to which these images are altered.

Although body image affects both teenage girls and boys, these issues frequently affect girls more than boys. According to the National Eating Disorders Association (NEDA), 89 percent of girls have dieted by the age of seventeen. Many teenagers report that they engage in dieting to try to avoid gaining weight or to lose weight. Teens may claim that they are dieting to get healthy, but the obsession with weight loss and obtaining body ideals can become unhealthy. NEDA reports that over one-half of teenage girls and nearly one-third of teenage boys control their weight via unhealthy behaviors such as "skipping meals, fasting, smoking cigarettes, vomiting, and taking laxatives." Girls who are classified as overweight are more likely to engage in extreme dieting than those considered more average in weight.

Dieting is one of the strongest predictors of developing an eating disorder. Eating disorders refer to unhealthy relationships with food that may include fasting, constant dieting, bingeing, purging, or a combination of these behaviors. The National Association of Anorexia Nervosa and Associated Disorders (ANAD) identified that 95 percent of people who have eating disorders are between the ages of twelve and twenty-five. Teens are one of the most vulnerable populations for eating disorders. Although girls and women are more likely to develop eating disorders, boys and men make up 25 percent of the people with anorexia, an eating disorder characterized by extreme fasting. Similarly, boys and men comprise up to 40 percent of the people with bulimia, an eating disorder characterized by bingeing and purging. Often, male eating disorders are undetected (not diagnosed or recognized) and thus are more likely to become fatal (leading to death). Eating disorders are dangerous and can result in numerous health complications. In a recent review of research, anorexia was the psychological disorder with the highest mortality rate.

Body image issues can be stressful for individuals who are experiencing body satisfaction as well as their close friends and families. Teens with eating disorders have more intense emotions or slowly withdraw from social situations that involve food. Coping with and supporting a friend who is suffering from an eating disorder can be very difficult. Parents and friends may attempt (but fail) to aid the teenager to accept and admit that their behaviors are unhealthy and indicative of an eating disorder. Teenagers with eating disorders often feel that these behaviors are necessary, and their obsession can make it difficult to see the problematic aspects of their behavior.

Teenagers may also feel embarrassed to share they have an eating disorder because of the stigma surrounding the issue. Currently, anorexia and bulimia are the most commonly underreported mental health issues. Family and friends can be essential for teens' coping with the stress of an eating disorder, but the recovery can be slow and difficult and requires guidance from an expert. Some clinical psychologists specialize in eating disorders and offer group therapy so that teens receive support from others who are suffering from eating disorders.

23. How does childhood trauma create teen stress?

Childhood trauma creates teenage stress because it contributes to more challenges and more negative feelings about stress, including avoiding reminders of the trauma, self-isolation, and hypervigilance (i.e., increased alertness). Severe hardships experienced as a child can alter the sensitivity of a teen's body to stress. Sometimes trauma increases or intensifies stress reactions, and other times, it dulls it. Simultaneously, due to increasing capacities for self-reflection and abstract thought, teens may begin to think about and confront childhood trauma but still lack sufficient coping skills.

In 2008, the APA estimated that 39–85 percent of children witness community violence, and 66 percent are victimized themselves. Sexual abuse is also considered to be common among 25–43 percent of teens. In 2015, the American account of child abuse and neglect victims was 683,000. Beyond these experiences of physically witnessing or experiencing violence, many children experience the death of a loved one; the chronic or severe illness of a sibling, parent, or close friend; or a natural disaster in their community.

The obstacles experienced during the early years and childhood are thought to have a powerful impact on psychological and physiological stress responses in the teenage years and young adulthood. Traumatic events are highly stressful events that generally have a higher potential for long-lasting negative effects. Children are still developing and depend on adults for survival. Particularly, their experiences of and reactions to stress are limited by their undeveloped, or lack of, linguistic ability to label experiences and emotions. Due to their lack of capacities, psychological defenses such as denial or dissociation play a large role in their ability to navigate the trauma. These factors create extra challenges for teens, especially as they gain the ability to reflect upon their experiences and gain emotional awareness.

Childhood trauma and the psychological defenses it requires often manifest into diminished focus, lower grades, and behavioral problems. Teens lack of focus is related to changes in biological stress responses, including increased alertness or focus on their environment and diminished energy or feelings of exhaustion. Childhood trauma is also related to dysfunctional self-concepts (identity) and more negative moods. Self-concepts are the views a person holds of themselves. Researchers find that as teenagers, victims of childhood trauma misattribute negative feedback or views from others as their own. In other words, they listen to and accept others' negative beliefs about them, including those that come from a friend, family member, or teacher. Their acceptance of others' harsh or criticizing views contribute to low self-esteem and lead teens to experience self-blame, loneliness, shame, and anxiety.

Relational trauma caused by neglectful or unstable caregivers and disrupted relationships (i.e., separation from parents) can lead to attachment trauma. Attachment trauma is an experience that leads a child to believe others are not trustworthy and that they are not lovable or valuable. This lack of secure attachment often leads children to recreate the relational trauma in their teenage and adult years by unintentionally seeking romantic partners that treat them similarly to their parents. Therefore, childhood relational trauma creates more relational trauma in adolescent years, contributing to more negative emotions, poor self-concepts, and insecurity in relationships, and all three contribute to stress. The insecurity in relationships impacts their ability to seek and find good social support to help cope with their emotions and problem-solve other challenges. Secure relationships involve both people feeling worthy and trusting one another.

Posttraumatic stress disorder is one of the potential outcomes of childhood trauma. PTSD involves intrusive reexperiences of the trauma (revisiting the difficult event(s)), frequent avoidance of pain, and the ability to be easily stressed. Recent reviews of research demonstrate that relational or sexual trauma may commonly lead to PTSD. However, this can include many other situations, such as the death of a parent or sibling, a fatal accident, the illness of a friend, or observing violence. In the childhood and teenage years, PTSD symptoms can include intrusive memories, nightmares, flashbacks, memory difficulties, jumpiness, difficulty concentrating, difficulty sleeping, reckless behavior, chronic pain, social isolation, irritability, or sadness.

Teens exposed to severe childhood abuse have demonstrated that they engage in constant error monitoring (staying aware of their behaviors in case of a mistake) and experience more fear, suggesting they may be anticipating stress. This can create to frequent nervousness. They can also experience a biological sensitivity or overactivity to challenges, which is related to mental health issues such as depression and anxiety as well as sleep disturbances and substance abuse. There are various forms of therapy recommended for PTSD, although the most effective form depends on the person. For children and teens, talk, art, and music therapy can all be helpful. Medication is currently not considered an option for preventing or treating PTSD, but it could be used to target symptoms, such as insomnia. Medication for difficulty sleeping or antidepressants or antianxiety medication for depression or anxiety.

Beyond PTSD, which is largely a psychological health issue, childhood adversity can have physical health consequences. The American Heart Association released a statement in 2017 that childhood adversity has been related to obesity, hypertension, type 2 diabetes, and heart diseases, and it has since begun creating important interventions that will create resilience in adulthood. In the teenage years, type 2 diabetes and asthma are physical health issues that may present themselves due to stress. Teens may also experience insomnia or struggle with poor sleep, leaving them susceptible to infections and diseases. Finally, childhood trauma victims use self-soothing techniques such as overeating, undereating, early onset drinking, and risky drug use to cope with the stress. These self-soothing techniques often become sources of disease in adulthood.

24. How does discrimination via microaggression and direct aggression cause teen stress?

Discrimination and microaggressions—the brief daily words or behaviors (intentional or unintentional) that communicate hostility or prejudice toward any group, particularly culturally marginalized groups—negatively impact teenagers' self-concept and identity. Discrimination is the act of using stereotypes or prejudices to treat individuals differently. While the experience of being treated as inferior or with hostility occurs to both adults and teens, teens are sensitive to these experiences in forming their identity. Discrimination can also occur via bullying or cyberbullying, creating aggressive or unsafe environments at school and harming teens' mental and physical health at home.

In 2018, the CDC found that being electronically bullied or bullied on school property was higher among female high school students (20% and 22.3%, respectively) than males (10% and 15.6%, respectively). Cyberbullying was reported as highest among white females (23%), Hispanic females (17.2%), and Black females (13.3%). School bullying was highest among white females (24.6%) and Hispanic females (21%). Yet, the study found that Black (9%) and Hispanic (9.4%) high school students were more likely to not go to school because of a safety concern than whites (4.9%). This concern was more common among females than males within each group. Of lesbian, gay, bisexual, and transgender (LGBTQ) youth, 34 percent reported experienced bullying on school property, 28 percent were cyberbullied, and 10 percent were threatened or injured with a weapon on school property. In addition to the bullying they experienced, blacks and Latinx teenagers are more likely to experience being pulled over or frisked by police than whites. A UCLA study of teen discrimination found that teens experience bullying and discrimination not only from their peers but also from adults such as friends parents and teachers.

Discrimination has become even more common via the internet. Research has found that children of color spend more time online than their peers. In a recent study, Brendesha Tyne, PhD, a professor of educational psychology at the University of Southern California, found that these children are subjected to viewing images of their community that are racist as one of the most common forms of discrimination. Up to 94 percent of youth of color have experienced some face-to-face or online discrimination due to their background. Children can understand racial and ethnic differences as early as six months old. However, they may not begin to understand the existence of stereotypes and prejudice as well as overt and covert discriminatory acts until middle childhood.

Teens begin to not only recognize and understand the existence of discrimination but also to contemplate the consequences that it may have for their life, including their identity. Within the teen years, it becomes possible to grasp the concepts of racism and privilege. This is because teens' brains transform to increase their ability to understand abstract concepts and to take others' perspectives. Because teens experience an increased sensitivity to social information, or what others think of them, discriminatory acts can have the most long-term effects in the teenage years.

According to recent research, the capacity to grasp the concepts of ethnic identity or gender identity and discrimination occurs simultaneously with the first signs of racial or ethnic disparities in health and well-being. In other words, the increased ability to understand discrimination in the teens years happens at the same time that scientists see differences in the health of those from minority and majority groups. Other researchers have demonstrated that minorities can experience a domino effect of issues, including discrimination, that ultimately interfere with their physical health. The domino effect explains how teens from minority groups experience more challenges in their daily life and, thus, more stress. Over time, this stress accumulates and creates biological changes that make it more difficult to recover from these challenges.

Additionally, discrimination can have more immediate impacts on stress. Tyne finds that teens experiencing discrimination face issues with problematic sleep. Teens within discriminated ethnic, racial, gender, and sexual minorities may also experience more prejudice that is directed toward their family members and community as a whole. This is associated with greater experiences of trauma. However, insults and other negative statements from other people, including teachers and peers, can create a stigma that diminishes teen's self-esteem by creating judgment about their identities. Identity development is critical during the teenage years; thus, these discriminatory experiences can interrupt the ability to find a stable sense of self that is essential for coping with stress and for decision-making.

A recent review of studies examining discrimination within teens revealed that discrimination was associated with more depression and withdrawal (isolation), poorer academic performance, and more hostility. This effect was worse among those who experienced discrimination in their early teen years. This is likely because teens often have not yet learned and practiced how to get help from others. Stated differently, they struggle to identify when they need validation or advice and from whom they should rely upon to get it. They often lack or are beginning to build other coping skills that may help them deal with racial, ethnic, or sexual discrimination, such as self-care. Thus, these negative experiences weigh heavily on their health. Research suggests that teenagers from minority communities frequently have less support from friends or less parental coaching, which reduces their ability to use positive strategies to cope with discrimination.

25. How does death and grief cause teen stress?

Teenagers' personal experiences of losing friends, parents, or siblings as well as their exposure to deaths around the world via the media can be mentally overwhelming and emotionally challenging, and this may lead to stress. The teen's closeness to the person who passed, the person's cause of death, and the degree to which the teen witnessed the death of the person determines the impact on stress. The grieving process, the emotional and mental experiences in reaction to death, can be especially challenging because of teenagers' sensitivity—it is often also called *bereavement*. Teenagers who lose a loved one to suicide, lose friends in a school shooting, or lose a parent to disease are more likely to experience PTSD as well as other mental health issues.

The sudden loss of a loved one and witnessing the death of a loved one have become the top two causes of trauma for adolescents. Approximately 3.4 percent of U.S. children are faced with the death of parent before the age of eighteen, according to the U.S. Census Bureau in 2001. The probability of losing a friend or a peer has also increased. The National Center for Health Statistics (NCHS) and the CDC report that there has been a steady increase in the rate of deaths among teenagers due to suicide and homicide from 2000 to 2017. Particularly, suicide among teenagers reached an all-time high in 2017. It is now the second-leading cause of death for Americans between ages ten and thirty-four years old. There has been a growing recognition of the potential harms of prolonged grief for teens. In 2018, the World Health Organization (WHO) drew from the *Diagnostic and Statistical Manual for Mental Disorders (DSM-5)* and included "prolonged grief disorder" within the *International Classification of Diseases (ICD-11)*.

The loss of a sibling, close friend, parent, relative, or caregiver can be especially difficult and overwhelming for teenagers. This is largely explained by their developmental stage; their bodies and minds are sensitive to their relationships. They are also gaining the ability to reflect on the meaning of life as well as the meaning of their identities and relationships. Therefore, a change to teens' friendships caused by the loss of a friend or sibling contributes to the stress teenagers feel. Many teenagers who have lost a sibling report that their friends felt uncomfortable and did not know how to interact with them afterward. The reduced quality of their conversations, the loss of positive interactions, and, often, their suppression of emotions increased their stress. Yet, research finds that the support of parents, caregivers, teachers, or friends who listen and support the teenagers in understanding their emotions appears to protect them from the negative impacts and stress this loss can cause.

Of the deaths that teens may experience, the loss of a parent can be one of the most traumatic—having the greatest effects on their mental and physical well-being. Social scientists who study the impact of grief for children and teens have found that teens who lose a parent often feel less positively about themselves (lower self-esteem) and their abilities (lower self-efficacy). This is expected to be due to the grief-created increased difficulty concentrating, restlessness, and fear. Research reveals that the majority of children that experience the death of parent do not later develop severe mental health problems. Yet, these teens can experience a strain in their relationship with the surviving parent or caregiver.

Because parental relationships are the foundation from which other relationships build, this not only impacts the mental health of the teenagers but also their future relationships. Later in life, the impact of this stress can manifest in issues with more alcohol- and substance-related (i.e., abuse of drugs) disorders, issues with intimacy, self-harm, and overall health complications. The risk factors are especially increased for teenagers from less wealthy and less educated families, as the loss of a parent increases economic challenges. The younger a teenager is at the time of the loss of a parent or sibling, the more likely it is to have a strong impact (see the question 23 about childhood trauma). Therefore, one of the protective factors is the relationship with parents and siblings, which can provide support.

The loss of a parent, sibling, or friend from suicide is associated with a greater risk of suicide attempts for the teenager who survives and experiences the loss as well. These teenagers are also at a greater risk for mental health issues and substance abuse. Research reveals that teenagers' grief can lead to more suicide ideation (suicidal thoughts), and it may prevent or diminish their sense of belongingness. Belonging is crucial for teenagers; thus, this loss important developmental goals for a positive self-concept or sense of self. Moreover, this lack of belonging increases their experiences of social isolation and loneliness, leaving these teenagers at risk for suicidal thoughts. The impacts of suicidal loss may not be immediate; research shows that parental suicide and bereavement often has a greater impact in late adulthood. These effects are reduced by appropriately engaging with psychological professionals and having positive support systems.

26. How can parental divorce or separation create teen stress?

Parental or caregiver divorce or separation creates teen stress because teenagers experience less safety in their homes, lose the freedom to be a teenager, and potentially feel that they will lose a source of support. Thus, divorces' and separations' effect on teen stress is complicated. It is often not the divorce itself that is most hurtful but rather the communication that surrounds the divorce and the relationships of the teen with their family members.

According to the CDC, a little less than half of marriages end in divorce in any year. This statistic has remained stable over the course of the last five years. Yet, originally, as divorce was increasing, it created a debate as to whether divorce is harmful for children and whether parents should stay together for the benefit of their children. Divorce and separation can both be outcomes of degrading relationships between parents or caregivers. However, they are distinct. Divorce occurs after there has been a strong commitment within the parental relationship: a marriage. However, birth parents may be separated because they had a child without the desire to be married and may have ended that romantic relationship. Parents may also remain married but separated.

There are many concerns about how a divorce or separation might affect the children within a family. There are often emotional, financial, and social consequences for the family. Many avoid divorce as a means to protect a child's or teen's well-being, by preserving a stable source of income in the family. Divorced women often struggle financially. Moreover, divorces require legal agreements about the custody of the children. Children, including teenagers, may be put in the position of choosing which parent they believe is more suited as a caretaker. Others may not have a choice or may find themselves in the middle of a fight between two parents. This causes their relationship with each parent to degrade. Sometimes, these teenagers are essentially forced into adulthood at an early age after gaining insight into the problems their parents face. These aspects of a divorce can be damaging to teens' mental and physical well-being.

Although divorce can be a catalyst for these issues, not all divorces are the same, and this does not mean that remaining married is better for a child. The pains of a divorce can be healed if the relationships between parents and children are maintained and stable. Therefore, it is more important to look at the communication between parents and teenagers to understand whether the challenges of divorce will likely be harmful to teenagers and whether teens can recover from this challenge or even thrive afterward. In fact, researchers have found that it is principally parents' inappropriate sharing that is psychologically stressful for teens. Teens experience a greater challenge when parents tell their children about the problems in their marriage or negative thoughts about one another. This is especially harmful if the teens are also exposed to frequent parental conflict or arguments. Parents who often have disagreements with one another and verbally blame and criticize each other may unfairly ask their teenagers for support. The demand of needing to support their parents while coping with the instability in their home is relationally unhealthy and mentally harmful for teenagers.

Research in the field of psychology has demonstrated that the relationship between parents is important for human development and can have long-term effects. The quality of the relationship between parents or caregivers has this effect for multiple reasons. First, parents model or reveal how romantic relationships operate and how people can love each other. Second, parental satisfaction and happiness in their romantic relationship can either energize or drain them, which ultimately impacts their relationship with their teen. Third, parents who engage in conflict regularly create an unstable environment. This unstable environment creates what researchers call "emotional insecurity," inconsistent levels of fear and concern. This emotional insecurity is directly associated with stress and health issues for teens who are exposed to it regularly.

This research suggests that parents who are in an unhappy marriage or relationship and therefore engage in more conflict within a home can not only increase teen stress but also have long-term impacts on teens. Nevertheless, conflict is an inevitable and healthy component of relationships. People in a relationship often have different goals or expectations. Conflict is not always detrimental. It can sometimes contribute to closeness by creating intimacy and facilitating learning about one another.

However, this research demonstrates that teen exposure to parental conflict is harmful because of the teen's uncertainty about who will take care of them. The teen may worry about their safety and resources. Parental disputes can also become overwhelming because the topics of conflict are often beyond the teen's maturity. Parental disclosures surrounding conflict (the way parents tells their children about their arguments) can also interfere with the teen's developmental goal of gaining independence from authority figures, such as parents. By needing to be involved in their parents' relationship, teens experience less independence. Thus, the conflict that precedes or comes before divorce as well the frequency of disagreements that occur during the divorce process can contribute to teen stress. On the other hand, parents who do not engage in sharing inappropriately about their relationship, who do not involve the teen in their arguments, and who do not argue in front of their teen can reduce their teen's stress and attend to their emotions about the divorce. This increased emotional security leads to fewer detrimental effects on the teen's health and future romantic relationships.

Finally, a component of divorce that may contribute to teen stress is that divorce remains stigmatized in some communities. This stigmatization may be experienced via social pressure or can be an internal issue. Stigmatization is the experience of thinking that something is uncommon and disapproved of in society. There are times when stigmatization is conscious and other times when it is unconscious. Teenagers may unconsciously believe in these stigmas and be ashamed of divorce in their family. This may impact their experiences as they begin to feel romantic and sexual attraction. The stressors of divorce can impact how teenagers view love and intimacy in their relationships by impacting the way they trust their partners. They may engage in such behaviors as avoiding relationships or being quick to judge their romantic partners, which can reinforce the pain they experienced with their parents. The impact on their romantic relationships can cause teens to lose self-esteem and to experience more negative emotions toward love and romance.

27. How does the need for privacy and freedom create teen stress?

The budding need for privacy and freedom creates teen stress by introducing tensions into teenagers' relationships with their family and adult figures in their lives. Teenagers' abilities to understand and label situations with abstract concepts allow them to recognize privacy and freedom. Yet, these concepts require exploring and can create internal conflicts that are challenging. They also create stress by leading to debates about when to ask for help and from whom. The search for privacy and freedom from family members is complicated by teens' exploration of friendship. They are only beginning their journey of learning when and where to trust others and share their feelings to get support.

Privacy and freedom are in fact abstract concepts that can take many concrete forms. Just mentioning the term *privacy* presents many different possibilities of what it means. What makes some information private?

And what does it mean to respect and maintain privacy? Similarly, *freedom* can have many interpretations or manifestations in reality. Freedom could refer to having absolutely no rules, it could refer to having control over decisions, or it could refer to the ability to ignore certain information. Privacy and freedom are complex concepts. They first become uncovered and desirable in the teenage years, but understanding how to navigate privacy and freedom extends far into adulthood. Privacy and freedom are essentially the realization of the need to create boundaries in becoming an independent and self-sufficient person. Boundaries are the expression of an internal affirmation of knowing what a person wants as opposed to what others want from a person. They occur when people reveal what they value and what they need.

Teenagers must begin to build boundaries with their greatest authority figures, their parents, but they do so while they are also exploring their own value systems. Thus, their boundary setting involves evaluating and recognizing when their values do not align with those of their parents. For instance, their parents may not value being a part of a sports team that requires early morning practices, but some teens do. Yet, it is common and natural for teenagers to find that their values—their preferences and views of other people and activities—fluctuate. Teens' evolving values can create confusion and arguments when they begin to establish boundaries with their parents. When teens are able to set boundaries that protect their time and energy in line with their values, they gain self-esteem as well as a more grounded confidence in their identity. Research reveals that when adults demonstrate trust and allow teenagers to create boundaries while also communicating their own boundaries, teenagers are less likely to experience poor mental health.

The setting of these boundaries marks a developmental transition from depending on and receiving the majority of support from parental figures to that of personal and social exploration. In these years, teens are focused on learning more about people their age and understanding how they fit in to their surroundings. They often begin to distance and differentiate their sense of self from that of their family and aim to become confident in their own identity and body. However, the desire to be independent occurs at the same time that teens face many new challenges.

While teenagers learn to navigate their own worlds, they rely on their friendships. Yet, their friends are limited in their ability to help each other cope with challenges. On average, their friends do not have experience coping with the new causes of stress, such as romance. They may be faced with similar problems and be frustrated from not knowing how to cope in healthy ways. Teenagers and their friends are learning important skills for decision-making, such as planning, considering consequences, and perspective-taking. Thus, they can struggle to empathize and offer emotional support to one another.

Meanwhile, the role of parental support in teenagers' lives is complicated by what Susan Petronio has called "privacy boundary turbulence." Petronio, PhD, is a professor of communication studies and the director of the Communication Privacy Management Center. She explains that when people change the way and amount of private information they share, they experience privacy boundary turbulence. Boundary turbulence is often interpreted as a threat to relationships (i.e., a potential reason to lose the relationship) and is generally stressful and uncomfortable. In the teenage years, parent-child relationships transition and are in a state of redefining roles with one another. They may not share information about their romantic or social lives or prefer to only share general rather than private information. Regardless, in pursuit of privacy and freedom, teenagers must create privacy language with their parents, siblings, and friends. They must also come up with tools to cope with the stress of potential privacy violations.

28. How does identity formation create teen stress?

The process of developing a sense of self or identity can be challenging. The lack of consistency and stability in a teen's identity can increase stress by making it difficult to make decisions. Thus, the successful and complete process of exploring and committing to an identity is vital for teens' stress, relational and academic success, and health.

During the teen years, between ages twelve and nineteen, the ability to think abstractly about concepts such as love and popularity develops due to physiological changes. Teens experience hormonal changes as well as transformations in the structure and volume of their brains in a region that supports their ability to think about concepts that do not physically exist. Although children can imagine other physical aspects of love, such as hugs and kisses, they can struggle to truly grasp ideas that are simply not physically observable, such as a belief and hope. Due to this increased ability, teens begin to reflect on themselves and develop an idea of who they are—their identity.

Simultaneously, teens also experience an increase in their ability to empathize with others, including understanding another person's perspective of a situation. The capacity to perspective-take, to think about another person's experience in combination with the ability to observe and judge oneself, leads teens to be self-conscious or worried about how others perceive them. At first, these beliefs about oneself are in a state of flux, constantly changing, but over the teenage years, a healthy teen develops a more stable sense of self.

This process was first theorized by a German American developmental psychologist named Erik Erikson. Erikson predicted that people experience eight stages in life. In each, they are faced with a different major internal conflict. Erikson theorized that during the teenage years, people are focused on identity development, or creating a sense of self and the roles one plays in their society. Their conflict is to have a single identity despite the many roles a person may play. In the process of clarifying their identity, teenagers are likely to find contradictions in their views and gain concerns about the ways others view them.

When teens lack a consistent or stable sense of self, also known as *identity*, they tend to engage in more risky behaviors, such as abusing alcohol and smoking as well as unsafe sex practices. Identity is essential to well-being throughout life, and teens are particularly sensitive to the instability of their identity as they gain self-awareness. The less consistent their identity, the more inconsistency teenagers are likely to experience in their relationships as well as in their academic life (i.e., school performance). These experiences create greater self-doubt, which slowly reduces the clarity and confidence in teens' identity.

Identity formation includes both exploration and commitment. During exploration, teens consider multiple options for the roles they can play and who they can be. Teens who are exploring may try befriending multiple social groups while they consider who they want to be. This process continues until they decide to commit to an identity. Over time, teens may come to reconsider their commitments to their values or to their roles and choose to discard or adjust them. In this case, they return to the exploration phase.

As teens enter adulthood, their commitments to values and roles, and thus their identity, become more stable. In this commitment phase, the chosen identity serves to help the teens make decisions by setting a path and standard for them. Whether teens are able to reach the stage of commitment influences their likelihood to experience stressful events and their ability to cope with stress. This is because having commitments to an identity supports decision-making processes and reduces internal confusion about what teens want and desire.

When teenagers do not reach commitments or remain in an exploratory state, they can begin to obsessively question their choices, feel paralyzed by their own self-doubts, and question whether they will ever meet their own standards. This process is called *ruminative exploration*. In ruminative exploration, a teenager can begin to feel lost. On the contrary, if teens have made commitments that do not facilitate a stable sense of self or are not satisfying over time, this also can lead to stress. In this case, they may feel not good enough and think that they cannot become a better self. Both are cases in which the identity developmental process faltered.

When teens' sense of self is incoherent and unreliable, their fulfillment and happiness with their identity suffers. They also face fears of not being capable of making independent decisions. The lack of consistency in their decisions and sense of who they are can also be a source of embarrassment and shame. Therefore, identity instability is associated with withdrawal from friends and academics as well as hostility and aggression. Teens may feel overwhelmed because they lack a specific value to help guide them in deciding how to spend their time. Do they want to be a good student who gets the top grades? Do they prefer to be bubbly and popular? Are they just a mean person? These questions about oneself can seem relentless and impossible to answer for teens.

Moreover, the lack of stable identity affects teens' coping mechanisms when they are faced with stress. For instance, teens with a clearer identity also tend to be more flexible in their problem-solving and are more likely to seek help from others. Research shows that teens who feel satisfied and clear about their identity free up mental space to evaluate more options when faced with a problem. With more clarity of self, they also feel less embarrassment and fear about a lack of independence, which leads them to ask for help. These teens use their commitment to values and roles to monitor, evaluate, and adjust their behavior. Therefore, they engage in fewer risky or unhealthy behaviors.

Teens with a coherent sense of self are better able to perceive obstacles in their life as a challenge rather than a threat. They approach difficult events as a chance to grow and confirm their sense of self. Therefore, stable identities predict better academic performance and resilience in teens. Ultimately, teens with an unstable sense of self often lack guiding values to give them a sense of growth and learning. This further creates inconsistencies in self-views and can later contribute to mental health issues. Teens' inconsistent identity creates internal conflict and contributes to arguments with their parents and their friends. The resulting relational instabilities can lead to hurtful exchanges in which friends, mothers, or cousins tell the teens they are "lazy," "uncaring," or "selfish," which may lead them to further question their self-view or commit to a negative self-view.

Identity formation can be complicated and confusing due to external influences. Ethnic and sexual identity can also play a role in self-esteem

and well-being. Teens who have bicultural identities or minority identities, such as identifying as black or Latinx or as lesbian, gay, bisexual,
nonbinary, queer, or transgender, may experience direct and indirect discrimination that leads to more negative self-views and more conflicts.
External pressures may create confusion or tension in developing a commitment to an identity. This is not only true at the societal level but also
at the family level. Parent-child or caregiver-child relationships and the
degree to which children are allowed to separate or become independent
people have a significant impact on their ability to successfully form an
identity.

Consequences of Stress

29. How does stress affect physical health?

Stress creates biological responses that impact the body's ability to produce energy, to protect itself, and to recover from injuries and diseases. Short-term impacts of stress include increased exhaustion, stomachaches, and digestive issues as well as susceptibility to viruses and flu. These physical health implications can interrupt and reduce the quality of daily life. Over years and decades, these physical responses can become more severe and permanent. Particularly, long-term stress can contribute to chronic fatigue, autoimmune issues, and heart or cardiovascular issues.

Robert-Paul Juster, Bruce McEwen, and Sonia Lupien, researchers at the University of Montreal, Canada, and Rockefeller University, have found that human's perception or experienced level of stress is strongly related to the level of cortisol in the body, the amount of stress hormone released in the body. Cortisol is released to energize the body, but if too much is released or if it is released for too long or too frequently, it has the capacity to slow down and prevent the immune system from performing its function. The immune system involves organs and tissue that protect the body from disease. Prolonged release of the cortisol hormone can diminish the immune system's functioning. When the body's immune responses are less reactive, this increases inflammation in the body. Inflammation is the swelling of portions of the body that are indicative of an existing wound or illness. When the body experiences inflammation, the immune system aims to heal it. However, the biological stress response of cortisol can block the immune system's ability to recover the body from inflammation.

Therefore, the length of time and the frequency of how often a person psychologically and physiologically experiences stress are important for evaluating their health risks. Although there are other physiologically reactions to stress, cortisol is currently the main biological marker that has predicted and explained other health issues. This is largely due to its clear relationship with the immune system. Research has found that resilient people and people who report experiencing less stress also demonstrate a quicker recovery in their cortisol to their typical state. However, others who struggle to cope with the cause of stress release cortisol for a longer duration. The longer the duration that cortisol is released, the longer the homeostasis or typical biochemical state is not met. Thus, the body is left in imbalance.

Short-term stress or thoughts of feeling overwhelmed that last between a couple weeks to a month lead to short-term increases in cortisol production and inflammation. Sometimes, as mentioned above, this biological stress reaction lasts longer than the conscious feeling or sensation of stress. When the body is inflamed and the immune system is slow to react, the body is more vulnerable to viruses, flus, or bacterial infections. Stress can lead to catching an illness because the body is not prepared to fight off— by producing enough white cells and antibodies—foreign bodies such as a virus. A person's physical health is therefore at risk.

Often, stress also impacts people's sleep such that they sleep fewer hours or have poorer quality sleep. This lack of sleep can intensify the physical impact of stress. Nightly sleep is a fundamental time for the body to heal itself from the day. During sleep, the body typically releases little cortisol, thus allowing the immune system to tend to inflammation and injury and reserve energy for the next day. When stress combines with little or poor sleep, any illness or injury that occurs requires the immune system to work harder and longer to recover. The longer this recovery takes, the greater chance the illness or injury will worsen stress.

Short-term stress can also affect other important body systems, such as the digestive system. The digestive system involves the various tissue and organs that contribute to human consumption and processing of nutrients as well as the elimination of material (e.g., food) after nutrients have been removed. Increased release of cortisol also interferes with digestion. The interference of the digestive and immune systems can lead to inflammation in the intestines and colon, which are the organs that absorb nutrients from food and eliminate the remainder. Inflammation can reduce the intestine's ability to take the nutritional value out of food, to process the food, and then to eliminate the waste, including causing diarrhea and constipation.

Another outcome of the impact of stress on the immune and digestive systems is acid reflux, the outcome of acid indigestion, which is identified by the acid from the stomach flowing up into the esophagus. Acid reflux can also cause a burning pain in the lower chest or nausea. When acid reflux becomes common, a teen may be diagnosed with gastrointestinal esophagus reflux disorder (GERD). The digestive issues of diarrhea, constipation, and acid reflux are treatable with medication available at a pharmacy or at most convenience stores, but these options offer temporary relief and are not cures.

Long-term forms of stress that impact a person for years or decades involve years of cortisol release and inflammation in the body. The consistent or long-lasting inflammation is associated with autoimmune disorders or underactive or hyperactive immune systems. These health issues include rheumatoid arthritis, inflammatory bowel disease (IBD), multiple sclerosis (MS), lupus, and asthma. Research has suggested that one effect of long-term changes in cortisol production is a poorly managed immune system such that the cells intended to fight off foreign or external viruses instead attack the body or the cells intended to heal the body do not react enough.

Research has similarly demonstrated that the prolonged presence of cortisol and inflammation increases risks for cardiovascular or heart disorders by creating changes in blood pressure. Blood pressure is the amount of pressure or tension within the arteries that is caused by blood. Blood pressure is measured when the heart rests and when the heart applies effort to push blood through the arteries to the rest of the body. Cortisol production increases blood pressure because it energizes the heart to beat faster and push harder while constricting the arteries. The Kaiser Foundation's study of stress as well as the Coronary Artery Risk Development in Young Adults' (CARDIA) study have found that more frequent and long-lasting stress experiences are associated with stroke at younger ages in adulthood.

There are also relationships between enduring stress and other major diseases. For instance, the studies by the Kaiser Foundation and CARDIA have linked enduring stress and physiological inflammation with increased risk for cancer in adulthood. Scientists are still examining the role of cortisol and the immune system in transforming cell production involved in cancer. Previous research has also found that those who have more long-term stress are more likely to have diabetes. Although releasing cortisol increases blood sugar temporarily to energize the body in reaction to a challenge, chronic and increased cortisol and blood sugar can be harmful.

Currently, the research does not evidence that stress causes type 2 diabetes or adult onset diabetes. Rather, it suggests the existing relationship between stress and type 2 diabetes is caused by emotional eating as a coping mechanism. Scholars have found that those with chronic stress who have imbalanced diets, including excessive alcohol or sugar consumption, are more likely to have poorer heart health. This suggests that those with lifelong or many years of stress may struggle to use healthy strategies to soothe their emotional pain, mental fear, and physical exhaustion. Due to unhealthy coping skills such as emotional eating, these individuals are more likely to experience future challenges and stress due to their diminished physical health.

However, the effects of long-term stress are diminished for those who engage in posttraumatic growth, or thriving. Posttraumatic growth, which is also called *thriving*, is the state of increased psychological and physiological capacity from recovery from stress. Research has found that thriving is often related to finding gratitude and appreciation for life and having affectionate and supportive relationships. Thus, people who experience long-term or chronic stress do not always have shorter lives or experience damaged physical health. There are tools and resources for engaging in posttraumatic growth that can protect people's health.

30. How does stress affect mental health?

The adversities and subsequent stress people experience can ultimately result in or exacerbate the symptoms or intensity of mental health issues. This occurs by impacting biological energy levels and responses to daily life situations. Specifically, the hypothalamus-pituitary-adrenal axis that produces the stress response can become disturbed or dysregulated with increased frequency and intensity of stress. The biological changes influence emotional reactions and, therefore, the mental health of individuals.

When faced with a challenging situation, the body reacts to meet the psychological and physical demand it requires by secreting hormones from the pituitary gland and adrenal cortex, creating cortisol. Cortisol plays a significant role in an individual's energy levels. However, when the body repetitively experiences stress, the biological stress response essentially gets less functional. It can be too sensitive and release too much cortisol or desensitized such that it releases too little cortisol. In both conditions, the body and thus the mind are less capable of coping with adversity. In other words, the experience of stress lasts longer than it would otherwise.

The physiological experience of heightened energy or deficient energy impacts the mind. In these moments, a less reactive cortisol reaction can feel similar to feeling too fatigued or low energy to cope. An overreactive cortisol reaction creates the sensations of the mind and heart racing such that is it difficult to focus on the cause of the challenge, existing resources, and ability to cope. Stress reactions demonstrate the mind-body connection. Frequently reduced or lower cortisol release in response to challenges can lead teens to feel as though they cannot deal with difficulty, thus lowering their self-esteem. Teens with an overreactive cortisol response, in which they feel overly stimulated by their life, can also slowly have more negative perceptions of their self. Research explains that these experiences can erode teens' belief that they can handle their life challenges.

The cortisol response is enacted in response to anything a teen views as a challenge. The body manages its daily cortisol levels such that they are highest in the morning and lowest in the evening. Frequent stress not only impacts the cortisol response to each experience but can also cause dysfunction in the body's routine cortisol levels, known as a *diurnal rhythm*, that affect teens' mental health. Research by scholars such as Andrea Danese, from the Social Genetic and Developmental Psychiatry Centre of King's College London, and Bruce McEwen, a neuroendocrinologist from Rockefeller University, have found that chronic or prolonged stress results in cortisol rhythms that neither rise nor fall, resulting in lower cortisol in the morning than is necessary to cope with daily challenges or a higher cortisol level than is beneficial. These changes have been associated with depression and anxiety. Often, these two can actually co-occur.

In 2011–2012, the CDC reported that 8 percent of teens have depression, and many of them (almost 75%) also have anxiety. Based on their dysregulated cortisol reactions, this means that the affected youth wake up every day with the sense that they cannot cope with their day, and they experience challenges for a normal sleep schedule. They may sleep more throughout the day or have trouble sleeping at night due to restlessness. The lack of regulation of their energy can create more challenges. For instance, the disruptions to sleep can lead teens to not perform well on tasks throughout the day and keep them from engaging in positive conversations, completing homework, and focusing on exams.

Thus, frequent stress increases the challenge of managing one's emotions. This includes making it more difficult to cope with causes of stress, such as chronic illness, abusive or unstable family, or discrimination and microaggressions. The reoccurring experience of maladaptive (not right) amounts of energy in response to stress can lead to more harmful coping mechanisms. These harmful coping mechanisms include avoiding thoughts, suppressing emotions, or ruminating, which is the act of repetitively thinking about the cause of their stress. These behaviors have been associated with an increased risk for eating disorders, anxiety, substance abuse, and depression. These increased physiological changes are also related to psychosis.

The two most common effects stress has upon mental health are increasing depression and anxiety—often at the same time. The existing research suggests that the frequent overreactive cortisol can begin to drain the body such that it "shuts down." The anxiety thus puts the body at risk for depression. Similarly, the lack of energy response creates other symptoms of depression, including a loss of interest in activities, such as spending time with friends; reduced self-care and hygiene; and diminished focus at school (i.e., poor academic performance). The reduced self-esteem can increase rumination and overthinking, and thus it can raise cortisol and create anxiety.

Therefore, the experience of stress can create a biological and psychological (body and mind) interaction that leads to mental health issues and disorders. These are largely a combination of having too much or too little cortisol, the problems this creates, and the effects it has on a teen's mind and emotions.

31. Could stress be harming someone's health even if they don't think they're stressed?

Stress may subtly or unknowingly have an impact on one's mental and physical health, even when one does not currently label oneself as stressed. People often experience symptoms that indicate they are stressed and do not recognize it. Stress affects people's biology and minds in different ways. Sometimes, people see a challenge or think something may threaten their well-being, but their body does not react with greater cortisol so they do not feel it. Vice versa, some people have greater biological stress responses but do not think there is a situation that is causing them stress.

To review, stress is not just an emotion nor something that only arises in thoughts; it has a biological component. Still, stressful thoughts can occur both more and less consciously. Psychologists have identified that thoughts and feelings vary how easily accessible and voluntary they are. Conscious thoughts are ones that people can easily direct or decide upon.

Other thoughts are less easy to reach or recognize, and some are completely hidden. The layers of the mind increase the complexity of recognizing stress. Some argue this is why meditation and mindfulness techniques are effective stress relievers and coping mechanisms.

Whether stress appears as exhaustion or anxiety can also differ across people, depending on their bodies and their previous experiences. For some, stress has an impact even when they are not conscious of its effects because their bodies have gained a hypersensitivity to stress. This is usu-ally due to experiencing multiple traumas and stressors throughout life. Thus, the signs of biological stress may not align with an experience they consider a challenge or threat. They experience racing heartbeats or sweating even when they do not think they are challenged.

Conversely, for some people, their stress unconsciously impacts their health because their body does not have a reaction to stress. Their lack of physical and emotional indicators, even when they may face a chal-lenge, may lead them to believe that they are not experiencing stress. Yet, research suggests that when the stress response becomes biologically blunted or less clear, there are potential cascading harms. Blunted stress responses often occur due to long-term or chronic stress since early life. The diminished cortisol or biological stress reactions may impact men-tal health because that person is consistently underenergized for daily challenges—they may think they are lazy or incapable of success.

Beyond this intricacy of the mind, stress can impact health even with-out conscious recognition because people may not be aware of the indica-tors of stress. They may note they are tired, irritated, or upset, but without the tools to acknowledge stress, exhaustion, stomachaches, tension head-aches, or catching a common cold may not appear to be related to stress. Gastroenterologists agree that people often undervalue the role of stress in their gut health. Digestive dysfunction, including frequent diarrhea and constipation as well as acid reflux, may be symptoms of stress. While they are often recognized as health issues, they may not become resolved without addressing the stress underlying the gut issue.

People's ability to recognize stress can also be limited by cultural expec-tations that have been passed down and create a standard of what circum-stances "should" cause stress. People may fail to apply the label or deny their stress because they do not want to feel it. In these cases, the impact of stress on health usually increases or gets worse. The lack of acknowl-edgment leads to fewer resources to be used and, thus, less coping to occur. In this case, the stressor often only gets more challenging. Avoidance and denial of the issue are associated with more aggression, more substance abuse (i.e., drinking alcohol or using drugs in unhealthy ways), and poorer mental health.

There are many reasons why stress may be unacknowledged within a person. The first step in overcoming a teen's stress is often helping them to recognize it.

32. Can stress be harmful for relationships?

Stress can be harmful for relationships, but it does not have to be. It can also be the way through which relationships grow and become stronger. It largely depends on how the two people are able to support each other, connect with one another, and cope with each other as sources of stress. Still, humans are social beings. While stress has an effect on each person individually, it can also have an effect on the people surrounding them, their daily conversations, and the satisfaction they experience within their relationships. A person's stress can affect their relationships because it can also affect the stress of the people with whom they have a relationship. This question explores how stress could lead people to experience conflict with friends and other loved ones.

Stress can spread across people. When people experience challenges or hardships, they may turn to others for their support as a coping mechanism; they often benefit from this. The valuable and necessary search for support or validation involves expression and sharing of thoughts and feelings. Sometimes it also includes asking people for advice or help. Yet, because loved ones deeply empathize, they too may experience the feeling of stress. Thus, via the act of caring, stress can transfer from one person to another.

As people share their stresses, they may begin to feel more and more overwhelmed with the problem at hand and with each other. Repeatedly talking about a challenge can begin to feel more and more impossible to overcome. This can be draining, and the relationship may begin to suffer. People can even start to feel like they do not like each other as much. They may feel so unhappy that they begin to avoid each other, choose to no longer speak with one another for a while, or end their relationship altogether. In this case, the stress became contagious and consumed the relationship.

Thus, stress contagions can create rifts or falling outs between friends and couples. Though the ability to share stress is often beneficial, it can be harmful if the stress is not met with good coping skills or if the challenge is too difficult for people in the relationship. It is possible to prevent or relieve the effects of stress contagions. The weight of this stress can be reduced by showing appreciation and gratitude for one another or by spending time together doing something you both enjoy. These positive emotions may be difficult when stressed, but they can also make all the difference.

Stress also transfers among people because adversity exhausts and depletes a person's ability to be more open-minded and creative. Thus, people who are stressed often see more problems and fewer options, leading them to become upset with those surrounding them. This can lead to conflict. Conflict occurs when two people disagree. Because stress wears down people's ability to think creatively, it can be difficult to develop or acknowledge solutions.

The aggression and frustration expressed in conflict can hurt and stress loved ones and strangers. This in turn changes the way they react too. In their hurt, they may withdraw or also become angry with one another, which continues to fuel the fire of stress. This also increases the stress of the friend, sibling, cousin, or adult who engaged in that conflict. They often become less open-minded and creative in problem-solving from experiencing conflicts. As these conflicts build up, they hurt and weaken the strength of the relationship.

However, there is good news. Experts on relationships have found evidence that relationships are not doomed due to conflicts caused by stress. The more appreciation, gratitude, validation, one-on-one time, and laughter shared between people before either of them experiences stress, the less likely they are to get into arguments with one another. Also, when people overcome stress together, they tend to feel closer, happier, and stronger than before.

33. Does stress lead to even more stress? If so, how?

Stress can create an inertia toward more stress. Researchers have found that the toll that obstacles have on the body and mind often leave people vulnerable or at risk for more challenges, fatigue, and feelings of frustration. The inertia toward stress is often the most powerful and least obvious when the traumas and challenges were experienced in childhood. In the early years of life, and in important developmental stages, including the teenage years, a person's adversity can have long-term effects in increasing the likelihood for future stress.

The cyclical quality of stress makes it a complex topic to study. For instance, the outcomes of stress often become the causes of stress. A traumatic event or chronic illness can expend and tax people mentally and physically. These threats to well-being then become likely to co-occur with new threats, such as reduced mental health—major depression episodes or panic attacks. They can create obstacles such as contracting infections or other physical ailments or illnesses. These causes of stress can lead people to engage in coping mechanisms that are later threats to their well-being, such as emotional eating or substance abuse (i.e., alcoholism or dependency on tobacco, opioids, or painkillers). Stress that is dealt with in unhealthy ways appears to inevitably contribute to more stress.

One theory, known as *cumulative risk*, explains how stress can build up, especially during childhood and the teenage years. Cumulative risk refers to the additive risks that are incurred via every experience of stress. This theory explains that there are two routes through which stress creates stress in the future: one is by creating more environmental risk factors, such as arguments or failed classes, and the other is through internal risk factors, such as increased sadness. Ultimately, it is argued that the interaction between the two explains how children and adolescents may experience negative outcomes such as poor social skills, academic performance, mental health, physical health, and behavioral problems.

Groundbreaking work in the area of cumulative risk was conducted by Vincent Felitti and Robert Anda, from CDC, in 1998 in what is famously known as the ACEs study. ACE refers to *Adverse Childhood Experiences*. In this original study, Felitti established a relationship between the number of traumatic events and challenges that a child experienced and their physical and mental health. Since then, many researchers have replicated these early findings. They have found that the types of ACEs differ across racial lines. White children are more likely to have a parent with a drug or alcohol problem in comparison to black and Latinx children; meanwhile, black and Latinx children experience more neighborhood violence and racial discrimination. Most clearly, ACEs are not a minority health problem. Regardless of race, children in these circumstances are more likely to experience future stress.

Chronic stress in early years is a troubling challenge for society. In a twenty-year study of children led by Leslie Atkinson, an expert in abnormal, developmental, and clinical psychology from York University, and colleagues revealed that the traumas experienced by the ages of five and six predicted the stressful challenges experienced at ages twenty-five and twenty-six. They concluded that the chain of risk, or chain reaction that occurs between one cause of stress and another cause of stress is especially strong for childhood traumas.

The environmental factors are perhaps the most outstanding and often unspoken factors that create cyclical stress throughout childhood and adolescent development. The socioeconomic factors (i.e., social status, family education, family income) that caused stressors in childhood appear to be related to future challenges, including poorer relationships, less support from community, lower income, more neighborhood violence, more mental health illness among friends and family, and greater drug use among friends and family. These led to increased risk for other traumas, such as the death of a friend or family member, long durations of hunger, or abuse. They are also at greater risk to experience isolation and have less support in emotional coping (i.e., validation and comfort) as well as problem-solving to cope with each of these challenges. These reduced resources for coping with stress make stress more intense and likely to occur.

The cyclical nature of stress can be daunting. It can feel dooming to those who have experienced childhood stressors. Yet, much of this research only speaks to the "average" experience of people who have childhood traumas. This is to say that this work is not predictive of a specific individual's experience but, rather, a way to understand the general trend. Additionally, a great deal of work suggests that positive relationships, especially with mentors, as well as optimism and hope can diminish the negative impacts of cumulative risk. Current research has even found that some youth who experience trauma actually thrive—they grow and are more capable of handling the stresses of life.

Resilience and Managing Stress

34. What can protect someone from experiencing excess stress?

While it is possible to prevent some teen stress, it is not possible *nor desirable* to completely prevent teen stress. Stress is not always bad. Rather, teen stress can contribute to learning and growth. However, it may be useful to consider ways of managing or thwarting *harmful* levels of stress, which may have more damaging effects.

The harmfulness of stress depends on how people view the obstacles they experience and their own abilities to overcome them. Stress can therefore be exacerbated by people's thoughts. According to Susan Folkman and Richard Lazarus's cognitive theory of psychological stress, stress is an outcome of (1) a *perceived* challenge or threat that creates a demand and (2) a *perceived* lack of resources. Therefore, thinking "I cannot deal with this" or "I will never get over this" can make a stressful situation and its consequences worse.

One way people can aim to reduce their stress is by being aware of when they feel frustration toward, sadness about, or denial of stress. These feelings make stress more intense. On the other hand, noticing stress, accepting it as a part of life and expressing it can make situations less stressful. In other words, one way of preventing some stress is by combatting the judgment of stress. Even if it is physically uncomfortable (including tightness of the chest or a fast heartbeat) or emotionally frustrating and annoying, stress is not inherently bad. Research has found that the ability to accept stress and recognize it as a normal reaction to many situations in life may prevent stress from becoming harmful to teens' mental health.

Because the perception of resources also contributes to stress, it is important to be aware of such resources as friends, family, counselors, tutors, medicine, and conversations that could help cope with the obstacle (see question 36). Some stress can thus be prevented by making a list of coping tools that can be used when facing a challenge. Some of these tools may be self-care oriented, such as eating regularly, drinking enough water, and sleeping well. Other tools might include making a support system list, a list of people or numbers that could be called or texted in case of an emergency or challenge (see question 35). With a coping tools list handy, it becomes possible to visually see the tools and resources a teen has to deal with challenges. Over time, a teen may even be able to recognize which tool they like to use the most, and they may become comfortable using more tools.

In the search for autonomy—being a unique individual—teenagers often wish to forgo their support from other people. It can become vital to teens that they tackle challenges on their own. For adults who care for teens, maintaining positive emotions, showing affection, expressing validation, and performing acts of gratitude can help teenagers prevent stress. Research has shown that building strong, meaningful relationships prevents stress and helps teens to view more experiences as challenges and not threats to their well-being.

The broaden-and-build theory reveals that when people have a reserve of positive emotions from their relationships, they are able to think in more creative ways to solve problems and are less likely to get into fights or arguments. Studies reveal that friends, dating couples, and families are more successful at solving their arguments and problems when they have expressed more gratitude to one another, shared affection, demonstrated more validation, and spent more valuable time together.

Researchers find that the ways of preventing stress also extend to daily personal behaviors, which includes the use of daily positive affirmations and expressions of gratitude. By expressing positive affirmations about oneself and appreciation for aspects of life, teens experience positive emotions. If done regularly, these expressions build on top of one another like bricks that together make a protective wall when struck with a problem. It can be helpful to engage in a daily form of humor as well. People are more successful at solving their own challenges when they have experienced more laughter and felt more positive emotions, including hope, self-confidence, and self-worth. These positive feelings increase teens' ability to thrive: to feel they have learned, grown, or become stronger after facing and overcoming an obstacle.

While stress is not completely avoidable, it is possible to avoid experiencing more constructive stress. In fact, there are ways of adjusting perspectives and preparing for stress that can increase the chances that stress becomes beneficial to people (see question 35).

35. Which coping strategies are useful for teens, and when?

Coping refers to the ways people react and aim to control their stress. Teens can choose to manage their stress by thinking positively about their experiences; by aiming to accept their experiences; by finding solutions to their problems; by seeking support from friends, mentors, or family; and by practicing distraction or avoidance. Each of these ways of coping can help teenagers overcome challenges and adversity. However, the degree to which they are helpful depends on when they are used.

Researcher Inge Seiffge-Krenke, from the University of Mainz, Germany, who specializes in adolescent coping strategies, found that at around fifteen years old, teenagers begin to refine their coping skills. These skills are often modeled by the people who surround them. Bruce Compas heads the Vanderbilt Stress and Coping Lab at Vanderbilt University, where he focuses on the ways that children and teens adapt to adversity. Compas similarly found that the new capacities, such as abstract thinking and the ability to think about thinking, known as metacognition, really begin to flourish in early adolescence. He noticed that adolescents may have tendencies or coping styles, but, in general, coping responses were a combination of situational factors and developmental changes.

The effectiveness of coping tools depends on a lot of a factors or aspects of a teen's situation. Not all responses to stress are helpful. The types of stressors are as varied as the best coping tools. However, there are types of coping tools teenagers benefit more greatly from practicing. These tools play a role in important skills, such as self-regulation and emotional regulation that allow teenagers to become adults who can adapt to more situations. Coping can happen on the thinking level, emotional level, or problem level (i.e., behavior) with either a focus on controlling the environmental situation or adapting to it and either engaging with or disengaging from the problem.

The complexity of the situation causing the stress may lead a person to use multiple types of coping tools for different aspects of the issue. For instance, for teenagers with HIV or who have experienced sexual assault, emotion-focused coping tools may be useful for dealing with the reoccurring pain it causes; however, if the pain becomes overwhelming, it may sometimes be beneficial to disengage and distract. It may be necessary to accept that one has the illness or that the assault has happened, thus adapting to the situation. Yet, it may also be necessary to control one's environment, such as seeing doctors regularly to prevent the pain from getting worse or preventing interactions with an assailant.

Emotion-focused coping deals with stress by examining the physical feelings and thoughts it has elicited, expressing labels for the feeling, and soothing these sensations. This can include meditation or mindfulness, relaxing, journaling to acknowledge one's emotions, or expressing experiences to someone trustworthy to be consoled. Mainly the goal is to accept, release, or reduce the intensity of the emotion. Problem-focused coping tools include seeking information or actions that could solve or improve the situation causing stress. For some teenagers or parents, this might include researching an illness that they have, such as diabetes; findings a means to leave a toxic environment at school or home; or finding an ally for protection from a bully or stalker. These two categories of coping are consistently considered beneficial. Importantly, previous research has demonstrated that both types of coping skills are impactful in developing resilience as adults; these teens are less likely to experience addiction or depression.

When using coping skills, teenagers cope with the source of stress by actively thinking about and reacting to it. In other words, they focus on the challenge. This way of coping can be beneficial, especially when used to express the emotions it causes or to reframe the problem. One of the ways to deal with teen stress is to notice and reframe teenagers' inner self-talk. Noticing all-or-nothing thinking or jumping to conclusions as well as other cognitive distortions or ways of thinking that tend to actually make teens' views of the world less accurate can be useful. Then they can adjust their thinking to accept stress and engage in self-soothing. Self-soothing is an extremely important coping skill in which teens must learn to engage.

Yet, there can be too much focus on stress. Rumination is the fixation or repetitive thoughts and feelings a person may have about a stressful situation. Rumination has been associated with PTSD. In disengagement, teenagers cope by actively drawing their attention away from the stress. Teenagers can actively disengage with problems as a means to try to cope emotionally or to solve the problem. This includes distraction from the issue, wishful thinking, avoidance, or denial. Typically, disengagement coping is considered less healthy than engagement coping, especially avoidance or denial, which are associated with emotional suppression.

Emotional suppression is the act of ignoring, not acknowledging, and not expressing feelings and thoughts. Emotional suppression, despite seeming like a tool for coping with a stressor, can often worsen the impact of stress. Researchers have found that teenagers who cope more frequently via disengagement also tend to feel more anxiety, aggression, or depression (e.g., withdrawal); have poorer academic performance; or engage in risky sexual behavior or addictive behaviors. These findings have led scholars to believe that avoiding a stressor ultimately becomes harmful because the impact of the stressor continues, but active coping can reduce the impact of stress.

A recent review of all the studies of teenage stress and coping has found that coping flexibility has the strongest relationship with reducing stress and symptoms of anxiety and depression. There is actually no single best coping tool for any one situation. There are some that are more likely to help. For instance, in the case of having a disease or facing the death of a loved one, the problem is not curable, but there are ways to reduce or at least not exacerbate the stress or emotions surrounding it. On the other hand, the stress caused by potentially failing a test may be resolved by getting a tutor, creating a study group, and studying. Thus, switching between these ways of coping and being flexible with using them in the face of various challenges is the most useful strategy.

36. What resources can teens use to help manage stress and crisis?

Depending on the source and intensity of the stress a teen is experiencing, there are different resources that could potentially help deal with the stress or overcome the challenges. These resources may be organizations, professionals, hotlines, applications, books, workbooks, or specific people that are together or individually useful for a teenager. However, knowing which resources to use and when to involve them can be a cause of stress too. Therefore, it is important to explore the available options and understand their potential value.

The value and impact of positive, supportive, and healthy relationships with friends and parents is immense. However, teenagers also have other options for resources. Each option may have a unique value depending on the type of stress. Research suggests that the more resources a teenager feels they have and uses increases their likelihood of managing stress positively.

Therefore, even visiting this question regularly can be a useful reminder that there is help available. It may feel like stress will never end or that a teenager is alone, but many people have worked hard to take their experiences and try to use them to help others who may have similar or worse situations. Even if a teenager's situation is rather unique, research finds that similar resources and tools tend to help them.

Trained strangers are a very powerful resource. For teenagers who are feeling intense emotions that are overwhelming them, such as fear and sadness, it is a great idea to begin the process of looking for a good therapist. A counselor, primary care doctor, or nurse may be able to recommend or help a teen find a good therapist. Yet, sometimes the personal beliefs of counselors, doctors, or nurses may keep them from recommending this option. In this case, it can be useful to keep asking questions to see whether their reasoning aligns with a teen's or parent's values as well as to explore the evidence for themselves. Some people's beliefs and cultural values may lead them to not seek therapy.

For those who choose to pursue therapy, it can take time to find the therapy or techniques that will be effective for them and a therapist that is a good fit. This may involve doing some Google searches, reading about therapy through *Psychology Today*, or calling one's insurance to find which therapists are within their insurance network. After choosing a few therapists to call, finding a good fit may include meeting with multiple therapists more than once. A good fit is someone they can speak openly with, leave not feeling judged, trust, enjoy talking to, and learn from. Thus, it is always a good idea to set up an appointment as early as possible; the worst that can happen is that the teen learns that they do not need therapy or the teen seeks another resource.

Therapy can be expensive, but there are often less expensive or free options at a nearby university, community center, or hospital. If it feels unsafe to look into these options or if there are no nearby therapists or clinics to visit, then online services can be a good option. Some recommended online therapy options include: Talkspace.com, BetterHelp.com, TeenCounseling.com, and PrideCounseling.com (for the LGBTQ community). For anonymous free counseling: text TALK to 741741, twenty-four hours a day, seven days a week, or visit 7cups.com or IMAlive.org.

In the case that a teen wants or needs to talk to someone immediately and anonymously due to bullying or cyberbullying, anxiety, or suicidal thoughts or they know someone faced with these issues, it is worthwhile to call the National Suicide Prevention Lifeline at 1-800-273-8255, twenty-four hours a day, seven days a week, even on holidays. If you are a Spanish speaker, call the Spanish-language Lifeline at 1-888-628-9454. *Si hablas español, llama a 1-888-628-9454. Lifeline orece 24/7, gratuito servicios en español.* If a teen speaks another language or prefers to speak in another language, he, she, or they can ask for a translator. Professionals are also available via chat at suicidepreventionlifeline.org.

For teens who are deaf or hard of hearing, they can use the Lifeline via TTY by dialing 1-800-799-4889 or use the Lifeline Live Chat service online. LGBTQ teens can also call the Trevor Lifeline at 1-866-488-7386, a free and confidential hotline that specializes in LGBTQ youth suicide. It will likely take under one minute for a trained crisis counselor to answer. The call will last as long or short as the teenager likes, but the professionals are trained to try to help as many people as possible. They will do everything to help come up with a good plan to help the teen. If a teen's life is in danger, they may need to call the police.

If a teenager feels their life is currently in danger (either by self-harm or another reason) or the life of someone they know is immediately in danger, dialing 9-1-1 to get an emergency responder is the best option. If someone has enacted a suicide plan or in the case of any life-threatening emergency, dialing 9-1-1, asking a close friend or family member to call 9-1-1 immediately, or taking the person to the emergency room can save lives.

These other organizations may provide more specific or tailored help:

- Teenagers who struggle with or think a friend may be experiencing addiction to alcohol or drugs may call the SAMHSA Treatment Referral Hotline at 1-800-662-HELP (4357). For free and confidential support for substance abuse treatment or for information, call the National Alcohol and Substance Abuse Information Center at 1-800-784-6776, twenty-four hours a day, seven days a week.
- Teenagers who know someone struggling with alcohol or drugs may also benefit from the Al-Anon/Alateen hotline at 1-888-425-2666, available from 8:00 a.m. to 6:00 p.m. EST, Monday to Friday.
- Teens who think they or a friend or sibling may have experienced sexual abuse or rape can call the RAINN National Sexual Assault Hotline, 1-800-656-HOPE (4673), for confidential crisis support.
- Another option for a teen in trouble who needs help is to text SAFE and their current location (address, city, state) to the organization 4HELP (44357) for immediate help.
- For teens in crisis, Safe Place, 1-888-290-7233, provides immediate help and supportive resources for young people in crisis through a network of qualified agencies.
- Teenagers who want more information about mental illness can call the National Alliance on Mental Illness at 1-800-950-6264 toll-free.

The confidential hotline operates 10:00 a.m. to 6:00 p.m. EST, Monday to Friday.

- Teenagers who feel they or someone know have trouble with food or an eating disorder can visit the website of the National Eating Disorders Association (https://www.nationaleatingdisorders.org) or call 1-800-931-2237.
- For trans teenagers, there is a peer support hotline run by and for trans people. Call the Trans Lifeline at 877-565-8860, available 7:00 a.m. to 1:00 a.m. PST, 9:00 a.m. to 3:00 a.m. CST, and 10:00 a.m. to 4:00 a.m. EST. Volunteers may be available during off hours as well. They also provide grants (money) for the process of changing a name or updating an ID.
- The National Human Trafficking Resource Center is available twenty-four hours a day, seven days a week. The confidential hotline is 1-888-373-7888 or text HELP or INFO to 233733.
- Teenagers who are concerned about or not feeling safe in their relationships can call the National Teen Dating Violence Hotline at 1-866-331-9474, twenty-four hours a day, seven days a week, or text loveis to 22522.
- For lesbian, gay, bisexual, and transgender youth support, there is the LGBT National Help Center, which provides the LGBT National Youth Talkline at 1-800-246-PRIDE (7743) with limited hours.
- For teenagers who ran away from home or who are homeless, the National Runaway Switchboard provides a confidential hotline that supports runaway youth for safety at 1-800-RUNAWAY (786-2929), twenty-four hours a day, seven days a week.
- Teens who are experiencing domestic violence or violence at home can also call the National Domestic Violence hotline at 1-800-799-7233 (SAFE), twenty-four hours a day, seven days a week.

Other resources include joining a club or starting a new sport or hobby to connect with new friends and gain support from others. Teens may be able to learn more information about their condition or situation from others and gain a place where their emotions are understood by joining a support group for teens. There are many types of support groups. They cover topics such as the loss of parent, experiences of discrimination, suicide survivors, dealing with diabetes, recognizing perfectionism, trouble with sleeping, coping with alcoholism, and connecting with others who are in the LGBTQ community.

Finally, teens can draw upon mentors. Mentors are people that teens admire that can help them understand their challenges and support them in accomplishing their goals. There are mentoring programs, or a teen may choose someone they already know from school, such as a teacher or someone with whom they work. Mentors can help come up with action plans and even act like a tutor.

37. When should teenagers consider receiving professional help for coping with their stress?

Teens should consider receiving professional support from counselors whenever their stress feels beyond their abilities or when they do not feel comfortable asking for support from their friends or parents. Professional help may be recommended when teens' stress leads to longterm anger or sadness; when their fears lead them to skip or stop attending school, spending time with friends, or enjoying their hobbies; or when they have frequent stomachaches or headaches. The likelihood that teens will seek help when they need it most is low; therefore, it is often the responsibility of caregivers, teachers, and family members to identify stress and suggest they get help. It can be worthwhile to seek professional help from a counselor or to speak to a therapist before it seems necessary.

A review of research on teens seeking professional help in 2018 found that only about 33 percent of teens with anxiety and up to 55 percent of teens with depression ask for help. Some even shared that they were unlikely to tell anyone about it. Teens may associate professional help with appearing "weak," being "crazy," or losing their independence. This may be especially true for teenagers who feel their parents are unapproachable due to harsh, controlling, or abusive behaviors. Teens who seek help generally have a more positive relationship or attitude toward therapy, counselors, and social workers. Therefore, it is important to keep an open and positive discussion about the option of receiving professional help for teenagers as a potential resource throughout the teen years, even if a teen does not display any concerning behaviors.

There are a variety of scenarios in which teenagers would benefit from professional help. Receiving professional help can be beneficial even before a teen's stress reaches the point of being out of a parent's or caregiver's ability to resolve the issue or support the teen. The help of adults who have been trained to help others gain emotional regulation skills and to support a healthy psyche can serve as a positive short-term or long-term coping tool. In these cases, the availability of a trained health professional is a resource that helps combat stress and increase teen resilience.

So, what are the signs that a teen may need professional help? Extended and frequent experiences of sadness, anxiety about being in social situations, exhaustion, inability to sleep, and a lack of desire to eat can be indicators that a teen's stress has become harmful. As stressors such as learning disabilities, moving, financial instability, or the death of a loved one become overwhelming, teenagers may find they are regularly tired, feel lonely or isolated, and are easily irritated or angered.

Teenagers should consider reaching out to a professional if they have repetitive or intrusive negative thoughts. These negative thoughts may escalate to the point that teens are consistently afraid: this fear may come from paranoia about external forces coming to harm them, or they may fear that they desire to harm themselves or others. Teenagers who find that these intrusive thoughts are becoming difficult to avoid and thus engage in avoiding others, self-harm, avoiding food, online violence, or overeating may benefit from counselors who can guide them through their stress. Thoughts, jokes, and threats of dying, such as "I wish I could go to sleep and not wake," "what's the point," or "I want to kill myself," are signs of a need for support from a professional. If adolescents are not experiencing tremendous stress, they would not have or feel the need to share these thoughts. Suicide attempt rates have increased in teenagers, especially among teen girls, but teen boys more frequently die from suicide.

Another instance in which professional help is beneficial is when teenagers experience stalking, violence, sexual harassment, or emotional abuse from the people they choose to date. In these cases, professional help may even include creating safety plans, figuring out the best way to communicate with the boyfriend or girlfriend when or if they see them again, or exploring the indicators that may exist in future romantic partners that indicate they are not a healthy choice. Because teens' friends may lack the experience and knowledge to support their friends after romantic trauma, and because they may not feel comfortable sharing it all with their parents, teens may be at risk or vulnerable to remaining in these unsafe situations or be more likely to engage in unhealthy coping. While seeking professional help can be challenging in these situations, not expressing the emotions teens often feel (such as sadness or shame) can make stress worse.

It may also be beneficial to reach out to a professional when the support of friends and family is no longer sufficient or if the teen largely relies on online support groups or online information about mental health issues. Teenagers may find that their environment is toxic or that their stress is heightened by their conversations with their closest friends, family members, or trusted mentors. Given the research that stress becomes exacerbated over time if not properly coped with, it is important that the lack of adequate support from these people be improved with help from a professional, such as therapist, psychologist, marital or family specialist, or social worker.

Similarly, when friends, family, or school members are concerned about increasing aggression or violent language in a teen's day-to-day life, this signals a teen could benefit from seeking professional help. Teens who have yet to learn healthy coping mechanisms often feel frustration with the cause of the stress, whether that is bullying or feeling isolated. Anger is a tool that many teenagers use to express the pain of stress. However, these behavioral problems are often symptoms that the intensity of the emotions has become too much. A professional could support the teenager in finding a healthy way to deal with these emotions.

Teenagers can also seek professional help if they feel that overuse or abuse of video games, smartphones, alcohol, marijuana, or gambling frequently causes problems for them at school, home, and with their friends. In these cases, teenagers may find that they are isolated from friends, perform poorly in classes, and engage in regular arguments with their parents. These experiences suggest that external support would be useful to help understand the frequent use of drugs, alcohol, or devices. It is a challenge for teenagers to break away from these habits, especially because it threatens their sense of independence. A trained professional can be helpful in navigating these challenges.

So, what can therapists do? Therapists and social workers are commonly misguidedly conceived as professionals that only provide diagnoses or listen to people vent. While they do listen and provide assessments for teenagers, their primary function is to guide teenagers in creating coping tools that minimize the gap between the intensity of the emotions caused by stress and the ability to respond to stress. Therapists have been trained in existing research and effective strategies for helping people. They often have experience with difficult situations and have learned more about the best ways to cope and overcome problems. Yet, if a therapist does not feel like the right choice, a teenager can consider reaching out to a religious or cultural figure.

There may be an existing stigma against or social disapprove for teens who seek out sources of help. This may be the most common reason why people do not reach out for help, but the only way to reduce the stigma is to talk about it. If more people share that they see a therapist or use medication, teens will realize they are not so different from one another. Teenagers who have a clear intention before meeting with a professional, enjoy conversations with professionals, and positively view professionals are more likely to receive the needed guidance. Thus, it is important to understand the signs that are exhibited when a teenager needs help and to also engage in normalizing the desire and process of seeking support, therapy, or medication as tools to cope.

38. When is psychiatric medication an appropriate tool for helping teens manage stress?

The use of psychological medication should be a choice that teens make with the help of psychiatrists and therapist who are mental health professionals. The usage of medication depends on the psychological issue or worsened mental health that is afflicting the teen. Families and teens should aim to increase their education and relationships with counselors, psychotherapists, or professionals, who help increase coping skills through talk therapy, as well as psychiatrics, who are doctors that gauge the use of medication for various psychological disorders.

In 2018, the Citizens Commission on Human Rights (CCHR), a nonprofit that aims to protect patients from abuse in the field of mental health, found that over seven million teenagers take one form of psychiatric medication. In 2013, 14 percent of teenagers had reported using a psychotropic medication in the last year, according to the *Journal of the American Medical Association of Pediatrics*. Importantly, many people believe that teenagers who use medication to cope with the stress of their mental disorders and illness will have lifelong relational issues or diminished success.

Medication can be a tool that allows teens to build important coping skills and may allow them to accomplish the extremely important developmental goal of having a healthy self-concept and developing independence. However, the use of medication differs depending on the challenge to health afflicting the teen, the degree of experienced suffering endured without it, and the recommendations of mental health professionals. Because the causes of mental disorders are still under investigation, the symptoms that denote mental health issues are also varied. Therefore, unfortunately, the process of identifying the most helpful medication can create more stress until it becomes effective.

The recommendations for whether and when medication can be an appropriate tool for teens is based on multiple factors. One factor is the teen's experiences, which may reveal detrimental experiences of symptoms of schizophrenia, attention deficient disorder (ADD), bipolar disorder (I or II), personality disorders, depression, and anxiety disorders. Another factor to consider is that teen's experiences of stress or trauma may be different from those of adults but nonetheless require extra guidance from health professionals as well as the support of medication. Importantly, distinguishing between the effect of trauma and disorders can be a great challenge for teens as well as health professionals. This is because teens' brains and bodies are undergoing tremendous change.

Still, one of the greatest challenges many teens' families face in recognizing the potential benefits of medication is their expectations, biases, and stigmas about mental health issues. For the teen, symptoms of a mental health issue can potentially overwhelm and consume their identity. They may feel a loss of their freedom caused by their poor health. They may also feel lower self-esteem. The monitoring of a teenager's mental and emotional state as well as proper medication usage can be conflict inducing between teens and parents. The potential problem is further complicated by the existing stigmas and internal confusion surrounding the use of medication. It can often feel like using medication affects one's sense of self and thus creates greater inner turmoil and stress. Still, the benefits of medication may be worthwhile.

Fears about the long-term challenges teens and their families will face due to mental illness can take great work to recognize as a teen or as a parent or sibling of a teen. However, existing work recommends that communication and having a select but varied set of options as well as a plan for decision-making allow the teen and the families to work through this adversity. Together, these can become unique and profound experiences that inform them about decision-making and identity, and they can create opportunities for connection between parents and teens. Medication can therefore heal teenagers and their relationships with their parents. This is especially true when family is able to embrace and encourage teens' sense of autonomy, validation, and trust even when they are questioning the "normality" of their experiences. Because teens are in a developmental phase in which finding their place in society and fitting in are extremely important and of focus, recognizing a disorder can be exceptionally hard.

Other factors to consider include being mindful of the mental health and pharmaceutical system. It is important to avoid self-diagnosing, pseudodiagnosing, or choosing medication primarily via surfing the internet, reading message boards, or watching advertisements. In these cases, credibility, trustworthiness, and motives can be difficult to assess. Seeing a mental health professional may take a long time to schedule, and it may take a couple sessions before a prescription or diagnosis is even discussed. Thus, when possible, it is important to consider the option of seeing a mental health professional earlier. It is possible, though not advisable, to cancel these appointments if a teenager changes their mind, but the key is to create options.

There may be instances in which parents and professionals will need to make the decision for a teenager to take medication. These cases should be reserved as responses to heightened symptoms, and timelines can be put in place to reassess. In these cases, teens are experiencing a limit to their most important developmental goal: autonomy. This can be especially emotionally and psychologically disturbing while their mind and body adapt to particular medications. Once medication is deemed necessary, this can be an additional stressor for caregiver and teen relationships. In this case, please refer to the question 4 in this book to read more about chronic stress.

Research by Robert Foltz from the Chicago School department of Clinical Psychology and from Johnathan C. Huefner's Boys Town National Research Institute for Child and Family Studies in 2014 revealed about one-third of teenagers have positive experiences with their medication. This may not be a large proportion of teenagers, but if medication can be a resource that will help them cope with the stress of their disorder, it is worthwhile. Still, the CCHR found that only one million teenagers are receiving treatment. Similarly, Mental Health America reported that, in 2015, only 62 percent of youth with a major depressive episode (MDE) were receiving treatment. This reduced level of treatment leaves teenagers at risk for increased symptoms and internalizing this into poorer self-esteem.

The use of medication should not be the first solution to symptoms of mental disorders; however, the research suggests that there are situations in which teenagers can truly benefit from their use. Significantly, avoiding the use of medication or meeting with a professional due to the stigma or fears teenagers and their families may experience toward mental illness may create more harm.

39. As a teen, how can you help a friend who's experiencing stress?

Teens can help each other when experiencing stress by acknowledging their friends' feelings, helping brainstorm ideas, supporting them in engaging in their plans for dealing with their stress, and listening to each other. Research demonstrates that friendships in which teens engage in healthy communication around stress protect teens from depression, anxiety, and academic burnout. However, the opposite is also true; when friends dwell on their issues or criticize one another, they decrease each other's self-esteem and create more social anxiety or a fear of interacting with people. Thus, friends can help each other through the way they speak with each other and by finding help from adults, such as teachers, counselors, and parents, when necessary.

In the teenage years, peers or friends gain significance and become the primary relationships. Scholars recently reviewed experiments and surveys conducted globally that examined how teens' helping one another impacts their mental health. The review showed that the help teens offer each other reduces isolative behavior, alcohol and drug abuse, and bullying and increases performance in school. These studies suggest that the acts of learning to share or self-disclose and creating close relationships can be beneficial to teens.

However, friends can range in their ability to uplift each other. Close friends and romantic partners who praise each other and offer each other validation and acknowledgment build trust in their relationships and gain self-esteem. They have more confidence in themselves and in others. On the other hand, when couples and best friends engage in negative behaviors, such as criticism, exclusion, pressure, and dominance, this can damage their feelings of self-worth. Even when friends have the best intentions, judging and pressuring one another can lead to victimization. Peers who feel victimized or hurt and belittled by one another can engage in aggressive and harmful behaviors such as bullying. Victimization increases fear of social interactions, diminishes self-esteem, and increases loneliness.

Teens best help friends by offering support via validating each other and problem-solving together. In other words, it is useful to tell friends that "you can see why they feel that way" and "maybe we can come up with some ways to deal with this together." When teens help one another, they not only help each other cope with issues but also help each other develop more empathy, compassion, and coping skills. Teens can learn from each other's mistakes in trying to overcome stress. For instance, they may learn that taking deep breaths is useful for dealing with the feeling of being rejected by their dream school or romantic interest. Thus, friends can not only protect each other from stress but also help each other develop responses to stress that reduce its harmful impacts. Friends who share their thoughts with one another and then try to understand the causes of their challenges are more likely to do this. This process is called *coreflection*.

One of the most effective ways teens can choose to help a friend during a time of stress is by creating an atmosphere that allows for self-disclosure. Social support becomes more effective when friends learn to trust one another and are able to honestly share how they feel. Self-disclosure not only includes sharing each other's problems or issues but also letting each other know when they no longer want to discuss an issue or if they are too stressed to offer support. Brené Brown, a psychology researcher at the University of Texas, Houston, has written numerous books about the transformational value of self-disclosure with authenticity and vulnerability. Through her work, she argues that courageously sharing fears, vulnerabilities, and shame with friends who connect on the issue can be powerfully healing. This healing is possible when friends allow each other to feel they "failed the test" or got rejected by someone they liked or looked awkward and offer how they relate to the experience. In this way, these self-disclosures decrease loneliness and symptoms of depression.

Teens can support one another through the challenges they experience by helping their friends solve problems and by offering emotional support. Scientists who study relationships have found that the best way to help a friend cope with stress may depend on the friend's personality and the type of adversity they are facing. Sometimes teens need someone to listen, and sometimes they want someone who will brainstorm solutions. Sometimes teens need someone who will help distract them from their pain or sadness. Teens who are experiencing acute stress as well as mental and physical health issues may need extra support. They can be limited in the support they can provide to their friends. In these cases, involving more mature friends or family members and considering the advice of an expert or adult can lead them to receive the support they need. It is important to remember that teens can only support one another if they are also taking care of their own stress.

40. How and when is it best for parents to offer support to their stressed teens?

Parents and caregivers of teens can benefit teens by offering them support before and while they are stressed. The majority of research demonstrates that parental support is valuable long before a child becomes a teen and experiences the unique challenges of that developmental stage. However, in reaction to specific teenage hardships, the best ways and times to offer support can depend on the characteristics of the teen, the existing parent-teen relationship, and the type of problem being faced. While parents' involvement with their teenager is often a protective factor from stress and harmful coping mechanisms, this can depend on how the teen feels about their parents getting involved.

Parental support's value transforms in the teenage years. Parents' ability to help relies on their ability to also embrace the developmental changes in the teenager. The teenager's next developmental goals are creating independence and identity—in essence, it is to carve out and claim their place in the world. In this process, the teen begins to focus on relationships outside of their immediate family or home. Parents may not be the most desired or powerful source of help, but they remain essential for teen growth and coping. Caregivers' unwavering support in invisible daily ways can often reduce the types and amount of stress teens face.

In support of this, developmental science researchers have demonstrated that the changes in teens' mindset are also seen in the parents' impact on teens' physiological stress. Developmental scientists use this biological change as evidence for the beginning of a new developmental stage. For instance, they have found that compared to the childhood years, parents' capacities to calm or placate their teens' physiological stress response (i.e., cortisol release) is less effective. On the other hand, friends' attempts to soothe a teen can amplify the physiological stress response. Teens' biological stress is sensitive to their social environment. Friends are a valued but challenging aspect of coping, as there may be additional stress in feeling dependent on friends. Still, research suggests that parents have less of an effect on the physiological levels of teens' stress.

However, parents can remain effective in their ability to reduce a teenager's *perceived* or felt stress by being a resource for coping with challenges. Scholars believe this is because stress is partially an outcome of a person's perceptions of their ability to overcome a challenge. Parents can provide instrumental support or their own resources (e.g., money to see a therapist, help with homework), ways to brainstorm or think through an issue, and emotional support (e.g., provide a safe and validating place to share emotions) or their nonjudgmental affection. These forms of parental involvement are effective when viewed as comforting by the teen. On the other hand, parental stress in reaction to a teen's adversity can often exacerbate the teen's stress. Parental frustration and sadness may be a natural response to their child's struggles, but it is important for parents to regulate these emotions. Using their own coping tools, parents can then communicate their emotions in ways that do not contribute to their teen's stress. This can create a calming yet authentic atmosphere for providing support for their teen.

Research regarding depression suggests that parents play a significant role in adolescent development and recovery from depression. Importantly, a review of the literature has demonstrated that parents can help teens apply coping strategies for overcoming depression, but this often requires that the parents learn and use these new strategies as well. This review revealed that there can be short-term benefits to including parents in the depression treatment process by holding joint sessions with the parents and teen. These sessions were successful because they improved positive parenting skills. Parents who seek their own treatment may be more equipped to support their teen.

Parental emotional support—validation and affection—can also boost a teen's ability to triumph over educational challenges at school. Gentle encouragement from parents can increase a teenager's sense of self-worth and self-efficacy, or sense of skillfulness, thus increasing their perception that they can conquer a problem. This perception impacts the level of stress the teen experiences and their ability to succeed. Multiple studies have found that teens who perceive more praise and reassurance are more likely to be resilient in the face of academic challenges. Emotional support is especially powerful as teens become more autonomous or able to take care of their own needs by learning how to drive, getting a new job to pay for their own meals, and even moving into their own means of housing. This emotional support is most effective when it exists before the stress.

Likewise, parental warmth, or the welcoming, nurturing, and affectionate expressions of care, love, support, and validation, helps teens who are experiencing stress. Frequent and consistent parental warmth expressed before challenges may cause some teens to feel less overwhelmed by their challenges. This is because it helps teens feel they are not alone in their problems. Parental warmth has been consistently related to less risk for teenage withdrawal or avoidance of parents and friends as well as fewer hostile behaviors. Therefore, one of the most powerful tools for supporting a teen through stress can involve engaging in positive bonding activities that demonstrate affection and gratitude. Parental warmth can change in reaction to teenagers' behaviors; thus, when teens withdraw or act aggressively with parents, this creates greater challenges for the parents. Parents may struggle to engage in these behaviors due to their own stress, but it is important to continue.

Still, parental involvement in multiple facets of their child's life can provide the teen a model for healthy relationships and trust that benefits the teen. Involvement or engaging in a child's life may include having open conversations, making rules, and spending time with one another. For instance, daily discussions about the difficult and rewarding moments of a day, having clear family rules about technology, eating one family meal together each day, and working on homework together are beneficial. As parents gain more information about their teenager's life from this sharing, they can often indirectly serve as buffers from challenges such as bullying and diminish the chances that these experiences lead to self-harm or suicidal thoughts.

Parental monitoring, or consistent checking and gauging of teens' behaviors, such as whom they consider friends, where they like to go, and how they complete their homework, can also be beneficial. Parental monitoring is most beneficial when parents also engage in emotional support and autonomy granting, or offering teenagers their independence. Parental monitoring can be harmful when it is an outcome of a lack of trust or a violation of privacy. Scientists have found that perceived parental trust and family belonging can lead to greater self-esteem and reduce the likelihood of engaging in risky behaviors such as substance use and abuse (e.g., alcohol, tobacco, marijuana). In these families in which teens experience trust and belonging, they also tend to have closer relationships with their caregivers or parental figures.

The theme underlying all these findings from research is that teenagers desire support and guidelines that demonstrate how to succeed, but they also need to experience autonomy. Without these experiences of trust and independence, youth often report having heightening stress reactivity and issues with withdrawal or aggression. Unfortunately, studies have demonstrated that when teens lack adjustment, many parents become more controlling, harsh, and authoritarian. These behaviors diminish autonomy and can sometimes thwart risky behaviors, but they may also create a cycle in which teenagers engage in risky behaviors that later lead to increasingly controlling parenting practices. In these cases, parents should seek professional help for their teens, themselves, and the family.

41. How can parents, parental figures, mentors, and caregivers help teens manage their digital stress?

Parents and caregivers may engage in a few tactics to help guide their teens' use of devices and help their teens manage their digital stress. They can engage in discussions about screen time or the content with which the teen engages. They can set rules and restrict the use of screens and engagement with content. They can spend time engaging in devices and content together with their teen. Beyond these three active and interactive tools for managing their teens' digital stress, parental figures can also engage in modeling healthy behaviors with digital stress.

The impact of the increasing amount of time today's teenagers spend with their smartphones, tablets, and computers has become a concern to many adults. The particular stress that is driven by engaging in these technologies has been referred to as *digital stress*. For teens, digital stress has two components (see question 7 for more information): (1) aggression and hostility and (2) the vulnerability of balancing their online and offline relationships and selves (see question 7). Through text message or direct message, teenagers can become exposed to cyberbullying at any time of the day or in any location. They also struggle with the demand from their friends to be constantly accessible and sharing their own lives and experiences to maintain their digital presence. These challenges are not insignificant.

Sonia Livingstone, PhD, one of the leading scholars of youth and media, has revealed that parental figures as well as mentors and teachers can support and protect their teenagers from the emotional burden, diminished sleep, and reduced physical health that digital stress can create. Parental involvement is generally beneficial in reducing teenagers' digital stress. In this endeavor, the most commonly used tool that parents have is time limits or content limits for their teenagers. This often involves barring teenagers from specific social media sites or applications, restricting the types of content they can post, and restraining teenagers from interacting with violent content (e.g., in video games or movies). The research into parents' use of rule setting suggests that its effect can be both positive and negative; negative effects occur when parents are hypocritical about rules without explanation or when rules communicate a lack of trust.

The other two common ways through which parents can help their teenagers manage and navigate their digital worlds is through active discussion and coviewing. Although active discussions and coviewing of digital media can occur separately, they often occur together and are both methods in which the use of screens and media content is enabled. In active discussion, parents and teenagers engage in understanding the reasons why they prefer the content they consume. They share when and where they most frequently use their screens. The purpose of active discussion is to connect with one another about shared experiences and then dive into thinking critically about the value of digital media.

Active discussion is the least commonly used technique alone, but across most studies it appears to have a positive effect on reducing the exposure to detrimental media content and subsequent stress. For instance, scholars have found that the quality of these discussions can predict the likelihood that teenagers feel addicted to their technology or become dependent on it for coping with stress. This work suggests that because digital media has become an essential part of life, the health of the relationship between parents and their teenagers depends on their ability to discuss it. One of the largest differences between active discussion and the restrictive ways that parents use to impact their teens' digital stress is in the reduced amount of conflict or number of arguments to which it leads. The conflict that digital media creates between parents and teens increases stress.

Similarly, coviewing has had positive impacts by reducing the digital stress that teenagers experience. In coviewing, teenagers and parents engage in digital media together: they watch their favorite television shows together, scroll through their newsfeeds, frequently text one another, and share their favorite videos. In other words, teenagers and parents connect via the digital media and incorporate it into their relationship. One of the most common ways parents and families have shared that this happens is by setting family media time. In these hours, families are able to use social media, games, and online videos to learn about each other and learn about positive uses of technology. These actions safeguard teenagers from the potential harms of digital stress by creating positive emotions with their devices and building trust between family members.

However, Karen Fikkers, PhD, and colleagues from the Center for Research on Children, Adolescents, and the Media at the University of Amsterdam have argued that the style or central message of parental involvement is more important than the ways in which parents aim to help manage their teenagers' use of media and consequent stress. In her work, she argues that these messages and styles of communication are the best predictors of how successfully parents can reduce their teens' digital stress. Fikkers identified three central messages that parents can communicate: (1) that they support, trust, and ultimately want the autonomy of their teenager; (2) that they aim to control and therefore condemn their teenager's behaviors; or (3) that they are unable to help their teenager. The first is more successful than the others.

In the first central message, parents can use all three tools—rules, discussions, and coviewing—but they use their language and behaviors to consistently show they trust that their teenager will be able to manage their own digital stress. They will aim to connect and understand their teenager. In the second type of central message, the controlling and condemning communication, parents often do not explain the reasoning behind their rules. Instead, they perhaps unintentionally communicate that teenagers would not understand them, undermining their trust of and in their teenager and expressing a value for obedience. Finally, when parents engage in inconsistent rule setting, such that they set limits but do not always enforce them, or inconsistent active discussions or coviewing, such that they set time to do so but are not fully present or are engaged in media themselves, this communicates a lack of ability to help to the teenager.

Jennifer Radensky, PhD, a researcher at the American Pediatric Association, has found that adolescents frequently say that their parents set rules that they criticize adolescents for not following, but do not enforce real consequences, or hypocritically do not follow themselves. In a recent focus group study, teens revealed that although parents may set a rule, such as no screens at the dinner table, they may break these rules themselves, which makes the rules confusing or less established. They shared how this discourages them to follow rules and ultimately leads to arguments with their parents. In Radensky's and Fikkers' studies, the inconsistency in the messages that parents express in helping their teenager can have negative effects that lead to increasing stress and risky behavior.

Therefore, parents have a few options in the ways that they can help their teenagers manage their digital media use and subsequent stress. The effectiveness of these tools relies on the communication and consistency that parents are able to express to their teenagers.

42. How can mindfulness and meditation help manage stress?

Meditation and mindfulness are strategies for coping with challenges as well as the physiological, cognitive, and emotional reactions to stress. They are effective because they allow teens to slow down their minds and bodies, leading to relaxation and better focus. From a calmer state, it becomes more possible to use helpful strategies to deal with stress, such as engaging in self-compassion, which is practicing self-kindness in recognition that suffering, failure, and imperfection are part of being human. However, meditation and mindfulness do not look the same for everyone.

Mindfulness is originally rooted in Buddhist and Zen practices. It involves activities of consciousness, or those that focus on attention and awareness. These activities, which originally had religious or spiritual traditions associated with them, are now commonly practiced in the United States for health purposes with no affiliation to religion. Meditation is one of many mindfulness activities. It involves learning to direct one's attention to the present moment. There are various forms of meditation practices, including sitting meditation, in which one focuses on one's breath or repeats a mantra. They can also involve other intentional physical movements, such as walking, eating, dancing, yoga, or tai chi. They can also involve applications (apps) such as Headspace or Calm.

Meditation is now often categorized as a mind-body therapy that allows people to practice relaxation processes and reduce hyperarousal to stress. Previous research has found that when engaging in mindful and meditative practices, people are able to decrease their blood pressure, heart rate, and sweat responses, which are indicative of stress. As the potential health benefits of mindfulness and meditation have become clearer, the popularity of these mindfulness activities has increased. A 2012 study found that 1.7 million children under the age of eighteen practiced yoga, and under one million practiced meditation. The National Institute of Health has stated that these practices seem to have promise for their impact on the public's health.

Mindfulness and meditation have also become popular in schools and among psychological practices, as they can impact mental and emotional functioning. Schools have involved them in their curriculum as an aspect of life skills. These programs teach children and teens to engage in activities that harness their attention or awareness to their internal states and physical surroundings. A recent review of studies that have examined the effects of mindfulness practices in schools found that including breathing, simple yoga, or body scans (observing the body from top to bottom) have consistent moderate to strong relationships with lessened stress and increased resilience. Those who engage in mindfulness report experiencing less stress in their life in general, psychologically overcome their challenges faster, and experience physiological benefits.

The impact of mindfulness and meditation is explained by their role in emotional regulation or the ability to notice, acknowledge or label, and adjust behaviors to manage feelings across contexts. Mindfulness training encourages emotional awareness rather than avoidance. It helps recognize that a person's thoughts, feelings, behaviors, and perceptions (or how they see the world) are related. It helps with identifying emotions and learning to notice potentially distorted thoughts that drive behaviors, such as yelling or socially withdrawing. Mindfulness can be essential to these practices by allowing teens to observe that thoughts and emotions are temporary and that they can be noticed without becoming overwhelmed by them.

Contrary to popular belief, mindfulness and meditation are not always relaxing. They may heighten feelings of fear or anxiety or increase clarity in hearing one's negative thoughts. Thus, for teens coping with trauma or PTSD, meditation and mindfulness can exacerbate their symptoms and thus should be avoided or engaged in given recommendations or guidance of a professional. Because emotional regulation is a challenge during the teen years, mindfulness and meditation training can be particularly effective in these years because the goal is to become more aware of feelings. Emotional dysregulation is associated with more experiences of depression and anxiety and other detrimental health outcomes.

Similarly, mindfulness's connection to self-compassion explains its powerful health effects. Kristin Neff, an expert in self-compassion, identifies three main components. First, self-kindness is the ability to be warm toward oneself rather than engaging in self-criticism and judgment. Second, common humanity involves recognizing that all humans are imperfect and that we all suffer. She claims this is a way to counteract a sense of isolation in which experiences happen to people alone. Third, she finds mindfulness, as opposed to negative reactivity to or the quick negative judgments of situations, is key.

There is a balance between not suppressing emotions and not exaggerating them or "overidentifying" with them. Overidentifying occurs when one situation is used to make conclusions about a person. For instance, if a person gets in an argument, they may conclude that they are an angry person; if a person fails, they may think they are a failure; and if a person feels lonely, they may feel that they are unloved. The three components of self-compassion become more accessible and more common via mindfulness and meditation practices.

Mindfulness's role in self-compassion has had strong relationships, 10 with a reduction in experiences of anxiety, depression, or stress. Teens that engage in mindfulness and, thus, self-compassion often have more resilience to stress. When teens are less judgmental of themselves, they experience less shame and do not experience mistakes or challenges as threats, reducing stress and increasing resilience. Other research finds that depression and anxiety diminish as an outcome of mindfulness practices because teens consequently engage in less rumination, focusing less on the past and less repetitively reviewing a past or potential situation. Rumination occurs when revisiting negative memories and supports more self-judgmental, harsh, or critical thoughts.

The power of mindfulness and self-compassion has been demonstrated among teens faced with various stressors. For instance, teens within marginalized groups who experience minority stress and practice mindfulness are able to better cope with stigmatized identities and were more resilient to the negative effects of bullying. Mindfulness, self-compassion, and meditation practices have also been effective for adolescents who are managing attention deficit hyperactivity disorder (ADHD) because they train attention and memory.

Mindfulness and meditation can be an effective way to increase teens' resilience and diminish their stress. There are many various ways to engage in and gain access to mindfulness and meditation techniques. Mindfulness could be mindful eating or walking, and meditation may be repeating a mantra while walking or eating. Today, there are multiple free applications that can be downloaded that provide guided meditation, websites online that provide examples or prompts for mindfulness activities, and online yoga and tai chi videos and classes. Various centers can also be attended to obtain support while learning mindfulness and meditation.

43. How can daily habits help teens prevent and manage stress?

On a day-to-day basis, there are habits that can help protect teens from stress and prepare them to manage it. While people cannot predict when stress might happen or may feel overwhelmed in the midst of a challenge, there are aspects of daily behavior that are important for stress prevention and management.

Daily habits such as diet, sleep, communication with others, and self-compassion affect the likelihood that teens find a challenge over-whelming as well as their ability to overcome the adversity they experience. Self-care routines can be an essential source of strength for physical and mental health through the transformations of teenage years. The schedule and nutrition of the food and water that teenagers consume on a daily basis are demonstrated to have strong effects on their energy and emotional well-being.

Some new studies suggest that the gut, or digestive track, almost functions like a second brain because of its impact on hormones. Eating healthy foods and eating regularly are essential for having the energy to cope with potentially stressful events. Moreover, diet has a large effect on immune functioning and inflammation, the process through which blood is supplied to parts of the body that are wounded or infected to help them heal. By affecting physiological health, hormones, and energy levels, diet is strongly predictive of stress prevention and management.

Similarly, the National Sleep Institute claims that adolescents require eight to eleven hours of sleep per night. When adolescents do not receive this sleep, which is essential for their development, they typically struggle with a skill they are gaining: self-control. The teenage years are important for learning how to monitor, evaluate, and change behaviors. Without proper sleep or diet, they are more likely to experience failures of self-control. This may manifest in a lack of awareness of their own behaviors and emotional states or a frustration with the lack of success in changing unwanted behaviors. Thus, teens with diminished sleep are at a greater risk for mental health issues, including depression and anxiety.

Daily media habits and uses of social media, the internet, texting with friends, and watching television can also play a role in teens' abilities to overcome the obstacles they experience. While some uses of media are good, research suggests the use of smartphones, tablets, laptops, and televisions late at night can lead to later bedtimes and poorer sleep quality. Thus, it is recommended that smartphones and tablets be set aside as a part of a good sleep routine. However, this can be difficult to do.

The National Sleep Foundation suggests that most teenagers do not sleep enough, they are up late studying or trying to find time where they can privately connect with one another without adult supervision. Thus, while forming the daily habit of not using media before sleep is best, changes to daily behavior can still help manage stress. When feeling tired and overwhelmed by life, it can be useful, at least temporarily, to value sleep over chatting with a friend about the problem.

In addition to diet and sleep, existing scientific examinations of stress find that positive communication in relationships is foundational to resilience. Specifically, expressions of gratitude, appreciation, and validation that are given to and received from valuable people serve as a source of strength when problems arise. These daily expressions with friends, family, and role models, whether said directly to the person or written in a journal, can boost moods. The positive emotions experienced can lead to more creative problem-solving and even lead to reframing an issue by remembering "the good."

Finally, the daily tasks of the teenage years can be frustrating. This period of growth in identity and independence are often accompanied by accidents and mistakes. Therefore, it is important that teenagers are accepting of the complications that are inevitable with growth. In a recent study, researchers Karen Bluth and Christine Lathren at the University of North Carolina at Chapel Hill and Michael Mullarkey at the University of Texas at Austin found that engaging in self-compassion protects teens from stress. Teens who are more forgiving of their own mistakes and engage in expressions of self-acceptance ("I'm doing the best I can" and "I know I made a mistake, but I will keep growing") are better able to overcome adversity and to approach their growth with openness, curiosity, and exploration. Thus, daily habits of kind self-talk support teens' strength too.

44. Can engaging in video games, TV, music, and social media be a useful coping tool for teenagers?

Digital media such as video games, social media, television, surfing the internet, and music provide teens a tool for connection, expression, and relaxation. In addition to other tools, media use can be a particularly healthy way for teenagers to deal with the stress. Social media can be used to generate a sense of belonging within a community, which can provide support. In moderation, listening to music, playing a game, reading a book, or watching TV can even be useful for disrupting negative thoughts or reducing pain. Beyond these uses, there are also games and applications that track moods and media usage or provide reminders to and rewards for engaging in healthy habits.

The Pew Research Center found that the majority of teens report using their cellphones to "pass time," 37 percent report using it to connect with others, and 30 percent use it to learn new things. Not all media are equally likely to be beneficial, but the statistics reveal that teens can experience benefits from media. In 2018, the Pew Research Center found three main benefits of social media: 81 percent of teens felt more connected to friends, 69 percent felt they were able to interact with a more diverse group of people, and 68 percent felt they have people who will support them through tough times. In Common Sense Media's survey of teens in 2019, 75 percent of teens who engaged in playing Fortnite reported feeling they had a positive experience, including bonding and making friends, handling challenges, and practicing communication. That same year, Common Sense Media also found that music is the most enjoyed media activity among teenagers. When and why do these digital media help teens?

Social media conversations can create semiprivate and accessible spaces to vent, plan, and gain perspective between stressful tasks. These spaces are important because the teenage years are an essential time between childhood and adulthood to gain independence. Therefore, online friends and communities can encourage healthy exploration and development of coping strategies. Online conversations can lead to self-reflection and perspective-taking, which create empathy and also normalize experiences. For instance, teenagers who identify as LGBTQ may find a community from which they experience validation (or understanding), receive information, and find people who can support them through challenges. In these ways, social media allows teens to manage their stress.

Research also finds that posting on or using social media to connect with groups of friends or clubs can boost teens' well-being and self-esteem. The photos posted and comments from loved ones on social media sites can have other benefits as well. In a study by Catalina Toma and colleagues at the University of Wisconsin–Madison, they found that reflecting on or viewing a personal profile can be used as a reminder about hobbies, achievements, moments of joy, and the support of close friends and family.

The positive emotions created by remembering and thinking about these other aspects of a person's life can act as a buffer against stress.

Beyond social media, research reveals that online video games allow teens to create meaningful friendships, reducing feelings of loneliness and isolation. When used in moderation, multiplayer online games as well as casual video games (or those that do not require advanced gaming skills) can be helpful for teens experiencing social anxiety, PTSD, and depression. These video games may interrupt negative feelings or provide a shared experience through which teens feel a connection with people and create friendships.

For adults and teenagers alike, listening to music—especially relaxing music—can physically reduce the level of cortisol (i.e., stress hormones; see question 1 on the definition of stress) and emotionally reduce the experience of stress. Music can be a tool for expressing emotions that teens want to process alone. Although music can be used to avoid or distract from negative emotions in a healthy manner, frequent use of music to avoid anger or sadness can aggravate stress. The same is true of television. Actively listening to music to feel emotions can provide relief and lead to acknowledging and accepting stress. Listening to music at night can also be part of a healthy sleep routine. Research has found that singing, playing an instrument, writing music, and moving to music are especially useful for releasing emotions and even reducing loneliness. Music therapy, through which professionals use music to help teens process challenges and trauma, can feel less invasive and yet more empowering.

Television can similarly help distract severely painful thoughts or feelings and create a connection to communities, friends and family, and role models. Scientists suggest an underlying factor that makes television helpful (as well as music, video games, and social media) for dealing with stress is the stories that are reinforced. Teens use television to deal with their stress because it helps identify, feel, or manage their emotions and think through their emotions and the scenarios they face.

The plot, mood, and characters in the stories told in television, songs, games, and social media posts affect the way people perceive their situations as well as their current emotions. Thus, it is important to remain mindful and intentional about the type of stories consumed; violent video games can be fun, and a dark television show about death can be interesting; however, they can subtly contribute to stress. This contribution may not be harmful, but in times of distress, it may sometimes be necessary to limit or manage how many disturbing, scary, or sad stories that teens consume.

Because devices and new media continue to define modern life, it is important to recognize the ways they can contribute to stress as well as the ways that help combat challenges. The benefits of music and games, for instance, have become more accessible than ever before. Yet, the easy access has also made them easy to use without even thinking, making it hard to keep track of the ways they are used to cope with emotions. Therefore, using applications that increase awareness or guide, monitor, and encourage healthy habits, such as exercise, time tracking on screens, mood tracking, and focus, are important to consider. Most of these applications have a free version, or they can be purchased for a low price.

As societies adapt to these technologies, teenagers and adults will together need to navigate these new challenges and, like many generations before, be creative in solving the problems they face—in this way, they create media resilience.

45. How can teens experience more resilience to stress and learn to thrive?

People often believe resilience is a trait with which a person is born: some people are born "strong," and others are born "weak." However, the existing research does not support this. Rather, scientists find that strength and resilience are partially explained by genetics and the family into which a person is born combined with the general environment, and partially explained by the person's exposure to and gained coping skills and resources. Finally, research has also found that teens can not only become resilient but also learn to thrive. Teens who thrive learn from their challenges such that they can cope better or handle more stress than before.

Teen stress is not *entirely* avoidable, and avoiding all stress is not desirable. Resilience to stress, as described in this chapter, involves the support, education, and wealth of one's family, a person's genetics, and their environment. This is especially true among teenagers. It also involves their responses to situations that reduce the likelihood of experiencing stress as well as their responses to stress that reduce its harm to the teenager and their community.

Teen resilience involves an ongoing and interactive navigation and negotiation between self, community, and environment. The process of negotiation involves learning what teens can expect and ask of themselves, their communities, and their environment. Resilience is about adjusting to and recovering from the various causes of stress that teenagers may come across. It is the return to a baseline over and over again as teenagers gain new experiences. Teenagers' internal baselines are hard to define because their bodies are undergoing changes and because they only have an emerging ability to reflect upon who they are and how they feel. Teenagers with more stable and consistent relationships with caregivers may more easily find or recognize an internal baseline. Baselines in childhood depend on the adults that surround children. Therefore, teens may feel less resilient than they are in reality.

Resilience is not the absence or lack of stress. It is the ability to avoid some of the riskiest adversities and, more importantly, to respond in a way that more quickly reduces the feeling of stress. So, how can teens do this?

First, teenagers are more likely to be resilient if they can acknowledge and accept the factors that are causing their stress. Part of strength is understanding when it is challenged and being able to accept this as a part of daily life. Teenagers who practice expressing and exploring the words to describe their challenges and stress are more likely to find ways to cope with them. The rejection of stress or the refusal to realize that it is happening, often out of the fear that it would make them "weak" or hurt them, actually makes stress worse.

Teens cannot completely control whether other people see them as "weak," but they can look for communities (online or at school) and people (friends, professionals, and mentors) who will acknowledge and support their stress. Teenagers become more resilient when they and their environment support them in saying, "Oh, I think I am stressed," "This happened, and so I am feeling hurt, angry, nervous, or overwhelmed" or "This is difficult for me." From here, teens will recognize stress as a natural experience. Accepting stress rather than stressing about the feeling of stress can be the first step in dealing with it, especially because people cannot or have very limited ability to stop and control most challenges, such as death, disease, and discrimination.

Second, more resilient teenagers are more likely to believe they can handle their stress using their own skills along with the help of their friends, community, professionals, and family. Sometimes asking for help and being independent seem at odds. Yet, the most independent adults are able to be healthy because they know when and how to involve the people around them in dealing in stress. One pathway to resilience to stress is through the way teenagers view their challenges and their ability to deal with them internally with the help of others. This ability involves the knowledge of when and how to use the resources around them (see question 36 to learn more). The feeling of being supported by their community, family, and professionals and the resilience of teens' communities, families, and friends are also essential to resilience.

Third, teens become more resilient as they are able to practice healthy coping. The first aspect of coping includes learning to deal with the emotions that surround stress. Emotional coping includes psychological support from a counselor, therapist, therapy group, or social worker; validation and support of friends, teachers, staff, and parents; meditation; journaling; writing music; and expressing feelings via any form of art. It can also include gaining perspective and changing the way they view the cause of stress. This can include identifying whether a teen is engaging in thoughts that tend to distort reality, such as mind reading, catastrophizing, or personalizing.

The second form of coping skills involve problem-solving skills. Problem-solving is the ability to think through various options and possibilities for how to resolve a problem or challenge. In problem-solving, teens identify the problem, figure out why it is a problem, and then think of a solution. This can and should involve other friends and family or trusted people who may be able to think more clearly when overwhelmed by stress. Problem-solving involves thinking about what resources (tools) a teenager has and how they can use them to end or diminish the impact of the challenge being experienced. Teenagers who are more resilient may think of more options or get help thinking of more options for solving a problem—it can be helpful to try to brainstorm at least five ways to deal with or solve each problem. They are also more likely to involve people in helping them brainstorm ideas or in deciding which to use. Good problem-solving also involves creating a plan for putting their tool into use, ways to know whether it is working, and identifying the next best option if the first choice does not work.

Scientific findings suggest that obstacles and challenges can actually be beneficial in creating a state of thriving. In other words, some teens responses to stress not only lead them to recover from stress but also to be stronger than they were before. Teenagers who learn to handle more stress actually grow more capable. Resilience is important to cultivate for teenagers, but thriving may be even more valuable. Resilience can become exhausting. It may feel like merely surviving. Thriving occurs when teenagers (and adults) learn from their adversities such that the next time they not only know how to handle them better but also find them less stressful.

The relationship between resilience and thriving is still a topic of research, but current science suggests that teenagers who experience trauma (the greatest stress) have the greatest opportunity to grow. Thriving teenagers are not only well adapted but also more successful than before. Teenagers who believe they can grow and gain skills or have a growth mindset are more likely to thrive. Similarly teens who aim to find meaning and purpose in their experiences of stress are most likely to thrive. These teens are not happy or grateful that they experienced trauma per se, but they often share that they are grateful for what they were able to learn through the experience.

Despite the limited research, teen thriving is included here as a reminder that stress is not purely bad and harmful. Research does not necessarily advise arbitrarily creating stress for a teenager, but it also certainly does not advise removing all forms of teen stress.

Case Studies

1. ANTONIO STRUGGLES WITH SEXUAL AND GENDER IDENTITY

Antonio grew up in a small rural town in Northern California in a highly religious Latino family. He has a large extended family to which he feels close; some of his family lives in Mexico, but most of them live in his hometown. Around the age of twelve, he began to realize that he did not feel the same as other boys he knew. His friends were flirting, texting, and talking about girls who they found attractive, but he did not feel interested in doing that. He remembered how at the age of six he loved wearing his sister's dresses and his mom's heels. He was beginning to think there might be something wrong with him. At the very least, he knew he was different and probably weird.

Antonio's family and friends made jokes and poked fun of him for not having a girlfriend. His friends often used the word *gay* to mean "lame" or used it as an insult. Even if it was a joke on their part, Antonio began to wonder whether they knew that this was true. Whatever he was, he felt it was not okay. He struggled with accepting his feelings; he worried he would be rejected by his family or create burdens or challenges for his siblings or caregivers. This frustrated him. He felt lonely and confused.

Recently, Antonio was in health class when the teacher had the students watch a video on teens and sexuality. After the video, the teacher asked the students about terms such as *gender*, *sexuality*, and *sexual fluidity*. He learned about the various forms of sexuality and the spectrum of gender identity. Sexuality ranged more than he thought: it included asexual, pansexual, bisexual, heterosexual, gay, and lesbian. Gender involved agender, bigender, cisgender, gender fluid, genderqueer, gender variant, transgender, and third gender. Many students were rowdy and not taking the video seriously. They used this time to text others. Some were even taking naps.

Yet, within the noisy class, one student was particularly brave—Tamar. Tamar proudly shared that she is a lesbian and that she felt this class was very important. At first, a few students insulted her and joked about her clothes. Antonio even contributed. But then another student opened up and said that they are nonbinary—they do not identify as male or female. He was shocked. Antonio had never heard anyone be open about their feelings related to their own gender and sexuality. He felt like maybe people would find him out next, but he also felt that he did not know how he identified and had never acted on any of his feelings of being different. Even though he never spoke up in class, he felt a strange pride for those who did and a little less alone.

After class, Antonio went home, and he felt an aching desire and a curiosity to learn more about his own sexuality and gender. He wanted to ask his teacher, how do people know, and when do they know? He did not know whether the teacher would understand. How does he decide, or does someone else decide? Does he have to decide now? What happens if he does? Will he lose his friends and family? Antonio did not feel comfortable sharing or asking in class, but he searched on the internet and began surfing social media to find more information. It was a bit overwhelming. He found himself excited but also scared. He read about people's experiences and different definitions online until late at night.

For a few weeks, this was overwhelming. It was hard to sleep, and he felt a strange quickening of his heartbeat and stomach pain before school. He found himself being nicer to Tamar, who had spoken up in class and shared that she identifies as a lesbian. He was struck by how normal Tamar felt. One day, she mentioned that she attends the LGBTQ club on Thursdays at lunch. Antonio wanted to tell her that he wanted to go, but he was too scared that his friends would notice and make fun of him.

One week, Antonio's friends were out of town, and Tamar invited him to join her so that he could sit with people at lunch. He said he would go to support her. So, he joined this club, and it was extremely eye-opening. For the first time, he was surrounded by people who felt similarly and had comparable experiences. He did not really speak up at first, but even so, they answered some of the questions he had worried about. He slowly began to feel freer and more liberated. He even found himself speaking without really thinking, and it felt like he could be open and honest about his thoughts without being judged. He felt like he was being himself.

Antonio did not return to the club regularly, but he secretly began reading more about the LGTBQIA community online and even watching some shows that involved gay and trans characters. He slowly began to feel that he had learned more about how he identifies. He still worried about what his family and other church friends would think about him if he told them about his feelings. This was a tension that created stress for him on a daily basis, but his growing relationship with Tamar, his aware-ness of the LGBTQ community, and his close relationship with his sister began to make him feel he could openly share his feelings through this process.

Analysis

Antonio is not alone in his fears of learning about his own sexual and romantic preferences as well as his gender identity. There are often chal-lenges and sometimes many conflicting feelings to knowing oneself. This is true for most adolescents, but these feelings and causes of stress are often exacerbated for those who do not identify within the binary gender traditions (male or female) or with their identified sex at birth or who do not prefer the opposite sex or gender. Many of these adolescents feel the same way and worry about how their family and friends might react to the discovery of their sexual orientation or gender identity. In the process of learning about themselves, teenagers may gain information at school, online, and from friends. This is essential because teens are less likely to be stressed if they feel accepted by others and find that there is a network of people who can validate and support them. Many junior high schools, high schools, and especially universities have support groups and classes that talk about issues related to sexuality and gender. There are also some 24/7 hotlines and accurate online resources for teens if they do not find information near them.

Importantly, research shows that accepting one's identity and coming out is a process that emerges over time. Adolescents often come out mul-tiple times to their family and may do it in different stages. For example, some teens come out to their siblings first, talk to online friends about it, rehearse the disclosure of their sexuality with their friends before their family, or tell one parent first before the other parent. Many parents are very accepting, but some are not—at least at first and others are not capa-ble of it. Research indicates that time often helps parents reach a place of acceptance. When parents and close family members are not able to reach this acceptance, teenagers often experience trauma, lower self-esteem, and reduced identity clarity. Yet, studies show the value of having a clear identity that feels authentic for teens' and adults' well-being. Therefore, identifying and accepting sexual and gender identity is essential for one's health.

2. TIFFANY AND ALICIA ARE FIGHTING

Tiffany and Alicia just started at a new high school and have considered each other best friends since they met in middle school. Tiffany and Alicia are often told that they seem inseparable. They are both in choir and theater, they take the same classes, and they enjoy spending time together during lunch and on the weekends. They also spend much of their time when they are not at school communicating with each other on social media. They text, send Snapchats of silly photos, share memes and videos, and tell each other about their days as often as they possibly can. They just get each other. Since beginning high school, the two have gained a larger group of friends that includes Amy and Sammy. Tiffany has also become friends with a new group of guys and girls through Amy, who knows the track-and-field team and the honors students.

For the most part, Alicia has been a really good friend to Tiffany. She supports Tiffany when she struggles with a difficult exam, cries with her over boys, and is happy for her when she does something well. Lately, however, Alicia has been acting strange around Tiffany. She has not been wanting to eat lunch together and acts cold around her—often texting "K," taking a long time to text back, and sending one- or two-word answers to the funny photos and memes Tiffany sends.

Matters were made worse when Tiffany and Alicia both tried out for a competitive soccer team; Tiffany made the team but Alicia did not. Alicia started telling Amy and Sammy that Tiffany was a selfish person who does not care about anyone but herself. While Alicia withdrew, Tiffany grew closer to Amy's group of friends, spending time with them on the weekends and attending events. Tiffany tried inviting her, but Alicia always declined and rolled her eyes, sometimes even saying, "It's not like you actually want me there." The things Alicia said continued to get worse. On Instagram, she commented, "Wow, imagine why Tiffany is surrounded by so many guys!" Later, she texted Tiffany: "It's like I don't even know who you are anymore. I hope you enjoy being a slut."

Tiffany was stunned and never texted back. Tiffany later heard that her best friend was telling people that she was "hooking up" with multiple people on the track-and-field team. She was devastated. She felt betrayed.

She began to confide in her other close friends, Amy and Sammy. Upon hearing Tiffany's story, Amy and Sammy were angry on her behalf. In fact, they said they did not care to talk to Alicia anymore either. Yet, after a chat with Alicia, Sammy began to ignore Tiffany. The two sat alone or often seemed to skip lunch. Amy's anger about how poorly Tiffany was being treated really made her angry too. Still, Tiffany felt like her whole world was falling apart in an instant. Her friendship group was split in two, and her best friend had betrayed her. If she could not trust her best friend to be kind to her, whom could she trust? Her grades and sleep also began to suffer because so much of her time and energy was spent focused on the situation between herself and Alicia.

Tiffany's and Alicia's parents began to notice the changes in their daughters. Tiffany's parents were very worried about her well-being. When they picked her up from school one day, she burst into tears and would not talk about it. Alicia's parents noticed that they no longer saw Tiffany and that Alicia was upset and uninterested in school. The situation got so bad that the kids were talking about Tiffany in chemistry class and belittling her. She told her parents about what was happening, and the parents then went on Tiffany's social media and through her texts. They felt like Tiffany was being bullied by Alicia and some of their friends. They took this situation to the principal, at which point Alicia's parents heard and became involved as well. They said Alicia had been bullied by Tiffany, who regularly excluded her from social events. In the process of all the fights between the parents, Tiffany was outraged that her parents and sister had looked at her phone without asking. Moreover, she learned that Alicia was likely going through something difficult; Alicia sat there crying while her parents fought with each other and Tiffany's parents.

Tiffany felt very low. She felt like her trust and privacy had been violated. She felt betrayed. She also felt sad for Alicia. The situation ended with both of them being suspended for a couple days and detention for a week.

Analysis

Navigating friendships and appropriately identifying and reacting to bullying are challenges for teens, especially in high school. During this time, teens are attempting to discover who they are apart from their parents by figuring out where they belong. Because of the increased intensity of emotions but lack of skill in labeling and coping with them, teenagers' friendships are often filled with more fights and arguments. Thus, friendships can contribute to an immense amount of stress. However, this is often exacerbated by the challenges of acknowledging and dealing with bullying, as seen in the example of Alicia and Tiffany. In these situations, it is tempting or necessary to violate a teen's privacy due to the potential harm and danger that teenagers are causing to one another. Still, it is important that parents do not let their own emotions become more important than that of their teens, and it is valuable to acknowledge the stress and pain felt by the violation of privacy. In this way, parents can at least validate and support teens through their stress.

In this example, Alicia was bullying Tiffany by threatening her social safety. She potentially mislabeled Tiffany's behaviors as purposefully cutting her out of her life. She was communicating out of fear and anger. Anger is often a secondary emotion to primary emotions such as fear and sadness. Alicia may have had trouble handling her emotions about another situation and felt afraid that their friendship was going to change or end because Tiffany made the soccer team and she did not. While arguments are part of a healthy relationship and Alicia's feelings are understandable, it does not mean that what Alicia did to Tiffany was okay or acceptable. True friends do not bully each other or put each other down. Both sets of parents were rightfully concerned about their child's mental health. However, they should have gone to Tiffany and Alicia first and asked what was wrong. They could have modeled healthier communication and focused on hearing both girls' feelings. If, after several attempts, there was no communication but the stress was increasing, the parents could have then asked to see the teens' devices to learn more. They could have also asked the girls to talk to a school nurse or called a confidential line just to talk about it, if that felt more comfortable. This would have given their teens agency and a feeling of independence while still providing support.

It is also healthy and beneficial to have regular check-ins about how devices make teens and parents feel. When devices are first bestowed, families benefit from discussing bullying and appropriate posting behaviors, sharing social media time or following each other's accounts, and setting rules about what happens when there is a concern for their well-being, including the right to check their social media accounts and phone. Research shows the most important and most challenging aspect for parents helping teens navigate social media and smartphone use is remaining consistent, active in discussion, and nonhypocritical.

3. HIGH SCHOOL IS HARD WORK FOR RICKY

After freshman year, Ricky felt he had succeeded in accomplishing his goals. Going into his sophomore year, he had landed a spot on the swim team and was placed in the gifted track at school. At his school, all sopho-mores get counseling about preparing for college. Ricky has begun to think about preparing for his SAT exam. He studies hard and takes a mix of hon-ors and advanced placement (AP) courses so that he can get into a good university when he graduates. Ricky and all his friends have been feeling the pressure to get good grades in their classes. They each make extra efforts to get ahead. Every day, Ricky gets up at 5:30 a.m. to go to swim practice. After school, he has more swim practice and swim meets almost every weekend during the swim season. After swim practice, he stays up late at night studying chemistry and completing his math homework.

Nights are an important time for Ricky. Weeknights can feel like the only time he gets to talk to his friends and catch up on social media. He is on the swim team and wants to go to college, but he also wants to have a social life. This means that he multitasks a lot, switching between home-work, texts, and social media. Sometimes this is useful because his friends will also discuss homework, class, or tests. Other times, Ricky loses track of time and ends up just scrolling and texting longer than he had expected. This happened just the other night when Morgan, his crush, texted him. He accidentally fell asleep and almost did not finish the homework he needed to turn in the next day. While nights are important for talking to friends, he also feels he needs time to relax. Ricky often likes to watch TV, spend time with his siblings, and listen to music while studying. He often finds that if he listens to music without words or carves out thirty minutes for his favorite TV show, it helps motivate him to complete his math homework.

Still, on nights before tests, Ricky can stay up as late as 2:30 a.m., leav-ing him three hours to sleep. Sometimes he gets in bed and all he does is think about his homework and tests. He eats sugar-filled treats and energy drinks to energize him when he wakes up. Sometimes, he and his friends even forget to eat lunch at school. Instead, they eat snacks from the vend-ing machine and consume more caffeine. They spend their lunch time asking their physics teacher about their assignments. Their time to do homework after school is very short or limited, so the teens would rather spend their time talking with their teachers about their last exam or fin-ishing homework together than use that time to eat.

Ricky's lifestyle became his norm. Yes, he was stressed on some nights before tests or days of swim meets, but he generally felt fine. Sometimes he even enjoyed the late nights and early mornings. The combination of late nights and the lack of healthy and consistent meals has begun to affect Ricky's health. He has lost weight and had the flu twice. His swim performance has suffered, and he has had a harder time staying awake during class. He has begun to spend even less time on weekends with friends because he has a lot of homework to complete to catch up to the class. On the weekends, whenever he is not completing his homework, he is often on the phone or using social media. This tends to create conflict with Ricky's parents, who ask him to put his phone down. His parents feel like they are constantly nagging Ricky to stop looking at his phone. Yet, Ricky insists that he needs to talk with his friends to do his physics homework.

Even though it helps him to talk with his friends about their homework on his smartphone, it causes problems when he loses track of time or gets distracted, causing him to go to bed later than expected. He also goes to bed with his phone, looking at it every evening as he goes to sleep. All of this makes Ricky even more tired in the morning when he has to get up for swim practice. Ricky thinks it might be because he's been sick and his parents have been fighting with him more often, but he realizes he feels more upset and annoyed recently. Is he stressed? Should be drop some honors courses or the swim team? Should he stop using his phone so much? What should Ricky do?

Analysis

High school can be hard work, especially because teens begin to manage multiple goals. In this case, Ricky, like many other teens, experienced stress from his effort to balance his social, extracurricular, personal, and school lives. Similar to Ricky, teens who aim to academically succeed can degrade their health through a lack of sleep or poor diet. This stress can result in frequent stomachaches, headaches, and colds. When experiencing stress due to school and time management, it can be difficult for teens to resolve the stress or to even recognize their own stress.

The teenage years are often the first time when an individual must make decisions about potentially life-changing decisions, such as college and finding good friends. These choices are especially time consuming and stressful because teens do not have a solidified or clear sense of identity. Meanwhile, they feel the pressure to perform well enough in classes to get good grades or to succeed and belong at school with friends. Although this stress is also contagious, such that teens tend to share this stress together, the harms of stress do not have to be. Adults can help by teaching teens coping tools and supporting them in practicing ways of coping. In return, this stress can help them grow to be more adapted and less stressed when they face a similar challenge in the future.

Ricky may benefit from practicing coping by examining his intentions and feelings when he engages in his current swim meets, social media usage, or homework. For instance, he could use applications that help him keep track of time (such as Be Focused or Forest) or use a bullet journal to help him track his tasks so that he can complete his homework in a more timely fashion. Parents and teens can engage in experiments to see whether adjusting how they use media reduces their stress. This can include trying to wait thirty minutes to read e-mails or texts in the morning, using a timer to focus on work for at least thirty minutes before switching to social media or responding to friends for five minutes, or unfollowing social media accounts that lead to FOMO. Additionally, it can be useful to plan healthy snacks or meals to take to school and to reduce caffeine, which may contribute to lack of sleep. Ricky may be able to cope with this stress by blocking out time, even fifteen minutes a day, for social and personal rest without technology.

4. KIM IS WORRIED ABOUT BEING ON HER OWN AT COLLEGE

At the age of twelve, Kim began to withdraw from her friends. Although she used to be talkative, she began to be quiet at lunch. She used to spend time at friends' houses, study with them, and go to the mall, but she no longer enjoyed it. One day, without saying a word, she left class in tears and went to the restroom. She did not want to talk with anyone and slowly became more and more frustrated with others. Her friends noticed her Instagram posts included quotes about how little others care and how the world is unfair. Her brother even found that she had written a plan to potentially take her own life. At this point, Kim's family and friends were concerned and helped her find help. She had to leave school for a month in eighth grade. Kim was so scared that she would not graduate. She was embarrassed to have to leave her friends.

Over that month and throughout her high school years, Kim met with a therapist once a week and saw a psychiatrist who diagnosed her with anxiety and depression. It took her until she was fourteen and a half to find a therapist that she really liked, but it was worth it. High school presented her with many challenges as she managed finding her career goals, completing her schoolwork, creating a sense of self beyond her mental health issues, and making new friends she trusted. These challenges were often exacerbated by her struggle to find the right medication. Some medication even made her feel worse. Yet, despite these difficulties, Kim completed her high school education on time with her friends and graduated with honors. She felt so proud of herself.

With the support of her therapist and because she had never been apart from her parents, Kim decided to go to college in a different state to see whether she could make it on her own. Even though she was looking forward to the next chapter in her life, she was worried about her ability to be away from her parents and handle college. She was anxious about being alone and meeting new people. For example, if she was not feeling well, would she do her own laundry? What if she forgot her medication? How would she manage to balance school and work? She was worried about her ability to find a job to help pay for some of the costs of her schooling. She was also anxious about something going wrong and living so far from her parents. Being in a completely different state scared and excited her at the same time. She had learned to manage her depression and anxiety rather well in high school, but what would happen with all the new experiences she would have in college?

Kim eventually moved to college. She spent the first week of school in orientation, where she got to meet fellow first-year students. She also stayed in a dormitory, where she had two roommates and an older student who was their mentor. This mentor showed them everything in the dorm and around campus. She also had a meal plan at school to reduce the worry about meals. Still, the first year involved a lot of stress. She sought to find a new therapist and psychiatrist. She was not sure she felt comfortable showing her roommates her medication, thus she decided to hide it for the time being; however, this added an extra anxiety every day. She was worried what they might think. Living with roommates, she wondered whether some of her coping skills, such as meditating or journaling, would seem weird, but she practiced them anyway. She decided she would explain herself if she felt she trusted them.

Meanwhile, Kim struggled with deciding on a major and picking a path. She loved her classes, felt so inspired by all the opportunities around her, and introduced herself to all of her professors outside of the classroom. School was challenging and so was her social life. Even though she was surrounded by so many people, Kim's fears, and sometimes even shame, made her feel lonely.

Yet, Kim was resourceful. She registered with student disability services, which helped her set up additional assistance for her exams by providing a separate room where she could take her exams and extra time to complete them. She also enrolled in group therapy, where she could practice healthy communication and process college with her peers. She was really grateful for both of these resources. With the support of her therapist and by searching organizations on campus, Kim found a meditation group where she could make friends. She also got involved in a club that raised money and awareness for mental health issues. This gave her access to a network of people who experienced challenges with mental health or who knew someone that did. Slowly, she began to explore more of her other interests, including joining the law fraternity, and she decided to major in political science.

Analysis

Kim is not alone. Many adolescents struggle with anxiety, depressive symptoms, and other mental health challenges. One of the challenges of struggling with mental health in the teenage years is that it can take multiple years to clarify the appropriate diagnosis and most effective medication. It is important to remember that this can be a normal experience. One of the challenges with experiencing mental health issues in the teen years is that it can interfere with, interrupt, or complicate their ability to create a clear and positive identity. These fears are natural and normal. In a transition, these fears and challenges are often exaggerated or made worse. Because teens are concerned with belonging, they are especially sensitive to stigma. While it is important that Kim was mindful about when she felt comfortable sharing things about herself and her mental health issues, the use of medication has become more common and widely accepted.

In navigating each of her challenges, Kim was resourceful. In the appropriate situation, telling a professor or friend could lead to validation and support. Therefore, using the local mental health specialists and seeking accommodations for her disability allowed her to figure out the norms and best ways to not only manage her own challenges but also how and when to share with others. College campuses often provide free or discounted mental health services.

5. DANTE DOESN'T FEEL LIKE HE BELONGS

Dante is usually confident in who he is, but sometimes he thinks that he does not fit in with any specific group at school. He came to high school with a set of friends he had known since elementary school and others since middle school. At first, he was really excited about being in high school with this group. In their freshman year, they became even closer, hanging out at lunch all the time and even making a few new friends that joined the group. They were really funny together. They could do anything and laugh. Plus, the group played dungeons and dragons and video games on the weekends, which he really liked. He enjoyed that they helped each other out in classes. It was just nice to have a group to sit with every day.

By sophomore year, Dante began to think that he might not like his friends as much as he used to because they were changing. After joining various summer programs, his friends appeared to each be finding a skill at which they excelled, but Dante did not feel the same. Moreover, he started to feel like he differed from the group. He felt tired or that maybe he had outgrown the activities they did together. This really began to bother Dante. He aimed to find some other friends under the advice of his cousins. In sophomore year, he joined the chess club and choir, but he found that he did not share a lot of other hobbies or values with those students. He did not watch a lot of movies or musicals like some of his friends in choir, and they did not play a lot of games outside of chess.

In his junior year, Dante decided to try out for the baseball team, but he did not make the cut. He worked on his form and practiced all summer, to no avail. His school had a requirement that you have to take a physical education class (P.E.) unless you are in a sport. Dante believed no one wanted to take P.E., because that meant you are not good enough to be in a sport. Dante tried out for the soccer team because he did not want to be in P.E. and made the team. He developed some friendships there, which were nice, but none of them were close friendships. They never spent time together outside of school. He also tried out for the mock trial team, but he came home sobbing because the tryout was humiliating. The team was led by attorneys from town who drilled him during the tryout. He felt stupid and as if he was not good enough for any sport or club. Did he need to make new friends? How was he going to make new friends? Where did he belong? He came home one day and threw his backpack on the floor, went straight into his room, and slammed the door. Even though he spent time with friends and had people to text, he felt he could barely call them friends. He felt lonely and frustrated.

Meanwhile, Dante's original friend group from middle school had begun engaging in vaping, drinking, and using drugs rather frequently. He felt that they spent most of their time either engaging in these illegal behaviors, playing games, or looking at social media. They really did not talk about anything valuable. He saw the path they were on, and he did not want to be like them anymore. Yet, he also did not feel that he had other friends. Dante wanted to have a group of friends with which to attend prom or to sit with at lunch. He wanted to stay true to himself, but he felt mounting pressure and sometimes chose to do things he did not like. Every time he gave in to peer pressure, he felt poorly about himself. But he was afraid of being left out or losing the friends he had. He already saw this beginning to happen. He found there were group chats that he was no longer included in and was sad to see all his old friends posting photos on social media without him. He was torn about why he cared so much when he did not want to be like them. He did not understand how his best friends had changed so much.

Dante struggled with many questions: What kind of person am I? What matters most to me? What am I good at? This was especially stressful for him when he began writing his college and job applications. He did not know what made him special or how to describe what he wanted. He hoped that he would be able to branch out and find more people like him in college. Yet, he wondered what those people would be like.

Analysis

During the teenage years, friendships and social activities become very important because they play a role in defining teens' identity. As teenagers struggle to establish their sense of self, they often try many different roles in their friendships and try to join various organizations to help create a sense of belonging. Identity, activity, and friendship and relationship exploration therefore occur together. Rejection during the teenage years can feel especially hurtful because of the lack of a solid and stable identity. Importantly, the pains and stress of friendship and identity have always existed, but they can be exaggerated by social media and the pressures of college.

Throughout one's life, friends are likely to change. The first termination a close, long-term friendship can be really painful. It may make teens uncomfortable to seek out new friends. It may take time to find good friends. Research suggests that in life we really need at least two good friends outside of one's immediate family and outside of any romantic relationship. Teens who have many friends may actually feel more stressed than those who have fewer friends because they need to manage more relationships and more identities. Rejection is a normal part of life, as is needing validation from the people around us. Rather than not needing others or completely depending on others to have a clear sense of self (define or know who a person is), becoming a resilient adult involves learning whose validation and opinion matters.

Glossary

Acute stress: sudden, usually intense or severe stress caused by a specific event.

Anxiety: the feeling of worry that can indicate a mental health disorder when a person's fear or nervousness becomes long-lasting and frequent.

Bullying: repetitive aggressive or hostile acts with the intention of inflicting harm on another person, which can create feelings of helplessness and fear in the victim.

Chronic stress: reoccurring stress that results from events or situations that are ongoing.

Cognitive appraisal: the way a person thinks about and judges their experiences.

Cognitive empathy: the ability to take on another person's perspective, to think about another person's experiences, and to consider another person's feelings.

Coping: the ways that people deal with problems or difficulties, which include reacting to emotions and problem-solving.

Cortisol: a hormone that regulates or manages the body's energy throughout the day and is released in reaction to stress.

Depression: a mental health disorder that involves long-lasting feelings of sadness and lost interest in activities that once gave a person joy.

Digital stress: the challenges that are created by digital technologies.

Discrimination: the act of using stereotypes or prejudices to treat individuals differently.

Distress: negative emotions that are an outcome of or about stress.

Emotion: a feeling or state of mind.

Emotional empathy: the ability to be sensitive and feel another person's feelings.

Emotional intelligence: a person's ability to be aware of, manage, and express their own emotions as well as recognize, listen, and respond to others' emotions.

Eustress: positive emotions that are an outcome of or about stress.

Frontal lobe: the part of the brain that is involved in the ability to think abstractly, plan, and foresee consequences.

Hormones: the chemical messengers that regulate people's bodies to impact growth, energy, the ability to reproduce, and mood.

Identity: the memories, relationships, and values that create a sense of self.

Inflammation: the body's way of signaling or communicating to the immune system to heal injuries or defend itself from viruses and bacteria.

Posttraumatic growth/thriving: the positive changes in perspective or skills that are an outcome of dealing with trauma or distress.

Posttraumatic stress disorder (PTSD): a mental health issue or psychiatric disorder that occurs in people who experience or witness a traumatic situation.

Psychiatry: a branch of medicine focused on the diagnosis, treatment, and prevention of mental health issues.

Puberty: the period in which boys' and girls' bodies change due to hormones, bringing about sexual maturity.

Resilience: the ability to prevent or overcome stress.

Rumination: repeatedly thinking about an event or situation.

Self-concept: a person's sense of self, including thoughts, feelings, and beliefs about oneself.

Self-esteem: confidence or general sense of worth a person experiences about oneself, which often fluctuates throughout life.

Stigma: a strong feeling of disapproval or negative judgments from surrounding people or society.

Stress: the mind and body's reaction to difficult, upsetting, or challenging events, experiences, or situations.

Therapy: a form of treatment involving talking, examining, and gaining insight into challenges with the aim of relieving distress and mental health issues; it is provided by trained professionals, such as psychologists, social workers, and licensed counselors.

Trauma: a very stressful, deeply distressing, and often disturbing situation.

Directory of Resources

BOOKS

The 5-Minute Anxiety Relief Journal: A Creative Way to Stop Freaking Out by Tanya J. Peterson MS NCC.

The Mindful Teen: Powerful Skills to Help You Handle Stress One Moment at a Time by Dzung X. Vo, MD, FAAP.

Put Your Worries Here: A Creative Journal for Teens with Anxiety by Lisa M. Schab LCSW.

The Stress Reduction Card Deck for Teens: 52 Essential Mindfulness Skills by Gina M. Biegel, MA LMFT.

Stuff That Sucks: A Teen's Guide to Accepting What You Can't Change and Committing to What You Can by Ben Hadley.

INFORMATIONAL WEBSITES

American Academy of Children & Adolescent Psychiatry (AACAP): This website helps identify when and where to seek professional help. https://www.aacap.org/aacap/Families_and_Youth/Resources/CAP _Finder.aspx

American Psychiatric Association: APA member physicians work together to ensure humane care and effective treatment for all persons with mental disorders, including intellectual disabilities and substance use disorders. http://www.psych.org

CDC LGBT Youth Resources: This website includes a resource list from the Centers for Disease Control and Prevention (CDC), other government agencies, and community organizations for LGBT youth to help support positive environments for all LGBT supporters. https://www.cdc.gov/lgbthealth/youth-resources.htm

Healthtalk: This website reflects the lived experience of mental health conditions, including research-based modules with hours of recordings and analysis. www.healthtalk.org/peoples-experiences/mental-health

It's Pronounced Metrosexual: This website provides a guide to gender identity terms and definitions. It explores both the common and uncommon terms that may be brought up in daily conversations about gender fluidity and identity. This list has been compiled by both research and reader input. https://www.itspronouncedmetrosexual.com

National Child Traumatic Stress Network (NCTSN): NCTSN offers resources, training, and educational opportunities that cover physical and sexual abuse; domestic, school, and community violence; natural disasters; and terrorism. http://learn.nctsn.org

National Eating Disorders Association: This website supports individuals and families affected by eating disorders and serves as a catalyst for prevention, cures, and access to quality care. Resources include quizzes for teens on body image and warning signs of eating disorders. Blogs and forums are available for teens to discuss various body image issues. This site is also monitored by a support team that can provide twenty-four-hour support to teens or family members that are struggling. https://www.nationaleatingdisorders.org

National Institute of Mental Health: This website provides easy-to-read guides and brochures to help better understand a variety of mental health issues. www.nimh.nih.gov/health/index.shtml

Psychology Today: This website has resources to help teens find mental health professionals and provides updates on research. https://www.psychologytoday.com/us

Substance Abuse and Mental Health Services Administration (SAMHSA): This website maintains an online, map-based program that visitors can use to find facilities in their vicinity. https://findtreatment.samhsa.gov

TeenHelp.com: This website offers resources for teens, parents, and professionals working with teens in a number of various health and social service areas. TeenHelp.com covers many areas within adolescent mental health, including stress, depression, and eating disorders. https://www.teenhelp.com

TeenMentalHealth.org: Geared toward teenagers, this website provides learning tools on a variety of mental illnesses, videos, and resources for friends. http://teenmentalhealth.org

ONLINE DISCUSSION BOARDS

Strength of Us (OK2Talk and You Are Not Alone): This is an online community designed to inspire young adults impacted by mental health issues to think positive, stay strong, and achieve goals through peer support and resource sharing. https://ok2talk.org/ or https://notalone.nami.org/

APPS

Addiction: Quit That!
Anxiety: Tapping Solution Meditations, MindShift CBT, CBT Thought Diary
Depression/Suicide prevention: notOK, Better Stop Suicide
Meditation: Headspace, Calm, Breethe, Insights Time
Mood and meditation: Stop, Breathe & Think, DBT Coach, Sayana: Thoughts & Feelings
Mood trackers: Daylio Journal, Moodpath, Youper, Moodnotes, Happify
Posttraumatic stress disorder (PTSD): PTSD Coach, Breathe2Relax

HOTLINES

Crisis Text Line: Text HELLO to 741741 for free and confidential support twenty-four hours a day throughout the United States.
Disaster Distress Hotline: People affected by any disaster or tragedy can call this helpline, sponsored by the Substance Abuse and Mental Health Services Administration, to receive immediate counseling. Call 1-800-985-5990 to connect with trained professional from the closest crisis counseling center within the network.
National Eating Disorder Association: Those struggling with disordered eating can call 1-800-931-2237.
National Suicide Prevention Lifeline: The Lifeline provides twenty-four-hour, toll-free, and confidential support to anyone in suicidal crisis or emotional distress. Call 1-800-273-TALK (8255) to connect with a skilled, trained counselor at a crisis center in your area. Support is available in English and Spanish. You can also access the Lifeline via live chat at https://suicidepreventionlifeline.org/chat.

TXT 4 HELP: Created by National Safe Place, this nationwide, twenty-four-hour text service provides support for teens in crisis. For information about how the service works, visit https://www.nationalsafeplace .org/txt-4-help.

Index

About the Authors

Nicole Neda Zamanzadeh, PhD, received her doctorate in communication from the University of California, Santa Barbara, in 2019. Her expertise and research focus on teen stress, resilience, family dynamics, and digital media use. Her work has been published in top academic journals within the fields of media, family psychology, and stress. Nicole has a decade of experience working with teens and has experience teaching courses from high school to graduate school. She has won awards for her teaching, research, and service to the community. When Nicole is not researching, teaching, or working with teenagers, she is likely to be found singing, dancing, painting, exploring the food around her, or watching the newest comedy, drama, or anime TV show!

Tamara D. Afifi, PhD, is a professor in the Department of Communication at the University of California, Santa Barbara. Her research focuses on communication patterns that foster resilience and thriving in families and other relationships, with particular emphasis on (1) how people communicate when they are stressed and the impact of these communication patterns on personal and relational health and (2) information regulation (privacy, secrets, disclosure, avoidance, stress contagion). She has received numerous research awards, and her research has appeared in many news outlets, including the *Wall Street Journal, Men's Health,* the *Huffington Post, Psychology Today, Canadian Living, Family Circle,* and OptionB.org. She is also incredibly passionate about teaching and has received several teaching awards. When Tammy is not researching, teaching, or engaging in service, she enjoys spending time with her family.